COACHING FOR Character

Reclaiming the Principles of Sportsmanship

Craig Clifford, PhD
Tarleton State University

Randolph M. Feezell, PhD
Creighton University

Human Kinetics

Library of Congress Cataloging-in-Publication Data

Clifford, Craig Edward, 1951-
    Coaching for character : reclaiming the principles of
sportsmanship / Craig Clifford and Randolph M. Feezell.
        p.   cm.
    Includes bibliographical references (p. 108).
    ISBN 0-88011-512-2
    1. Sportsmanship--Study and teaching.   2. Coaching (Athletics)-
-Moral and ethical aspects.   I. Feezell, Randolph M., 1950-
II. Title.
GV706.3.C55   1997
796'.07'7--dc21

                                                            97-9534
                                                            CIP

ISBN: 0-88011-512-2

Copyright © 1997 by Human Kinetics Publishers, Inc.

Acquisitions Editor: Jim Kestner; **Developmental Editors:** Marni Basic and Jan Colarusso Seeley; **Assistant Editors:** John Wentworth and Henry Woolsey; **Editorial Assistant:** Amy Carnes; **Copyeditor:** Bonnie Pettifor; **Proofreader:** Erin Cler; **Graphic Designer:** Robert Reuther; **Graphic Artist:** Angela K. Snyder; **Photo Editor:** Boyd LaFoon; **Cover Designer:** Jack Davis; **Photographer (cover):** Anthony Neste; **Printer:** United Graphics

Printed in the United States of America   10   9   8   7   6   5   4

Human Kinetics
Web site: http://www.humankinetics.com/

United States: Human Kinetics, P.O. Box 5076, Champaign, IL 61825-5076
1-800-747-4457
e-mail: humank@hkusa.com

Canada: Human Kinetics, 475 Devonshire Road, Unit 100, Windsor, ON N8Y 2L5
1-800-465-7301 (in Canada only)
e-mail: humank@hkcanada.com

Europe: Human Kinetics, P.O. Box IW14, Leeds LS16 6TR, United Kingdom
+44 (0)113-278 1708
e-mail: humank@hkeurope.com

Australia: Human Kinetics, 57A Price Avenue, Lower Mitcham, South Australia 5062
(08) 82771555
e-mail: liahka@senet.com.au

New Zealand: Human Kinetics, P.O. Box 105-231, Auckland Central
09-523-3462
e-mail: humank@hknewz.com

Contents

Preface

It seemed inevitable that we would write this book. Anytime we talked, the conversation would turn to the topic of sport—and then, inevitably, to sportsmanship. We talked about trying to teach it to the kids we were coaching and the kids we were raising; we talked about watching its occasional display and its frequent absence in college and professional athletics. Expressions like "respect for the game," "respect for the opponent," "respect for officials," repeatedly surfaced. We apologized to each other for invoking sportsmanship clichés in our conversations, until one day we realized that expressions that sound like clichés to us many young athletes today *have never heard*.

Twenty years ago Gerald Ford remarked:

> *Broadly speaking, outside of a national character and an educated society, there are few things more important to a country's growth and well-being than competitive athletics. If it is a cliché to say athletics build character as well as muscle, then I subscribe to the cliché.* (Ford, p. 247)

A generation ago many people might have nodded approvingly when such views were expressed. Twenty years later it is difficult to be as charitable when thinking about the moral possibilities of sport participation. What are our children learning as they turn off ESPN and hurry off to practice? There was a time when they may have had the good fortune of watching Mickey Mantle trot around the bases after hitting a home run, head down so as not to show up the opposing pitcher, exhibiting a respect for his opponent and a humility and grace in relation to the traditions and reality of the game of baseball. Now what do they learn when they watch sports on TV? Respect for opponents? Humility? Grace? Loyalty? Hardly. It would be tedious to recite a lengthy list of the disturbing aspects of contemporary sports: bench-clearing brawls, trash talking, taunting, strutting, college athletic scandals, cheating, drug abuse—why go on?

A cover story by columnist Robert Lipsyte in the April 2, 1995 issue of *The New York Times Magazine* even proclaims the end of American sports:

> *Sports are over because they no longer have any moral resonance. They are merely entertainment, the bread and circuses of a New Rome. Nothing*

makes this more chillingly real than our current Babes: Mike Tyson and Tonya Harding. Two of the neediest, hungriest, most troubled and misguided young people in athletic history, they are the archetypal extremes of this frenzied, confused sports endgame. (p. 56)

But merely bemoaning the situation is not enough. Something seems to have happened concerning the substance of our collective moral lives, in sports and in society at large—and some kind of response is called for. Indeed, the proliferation of recent responses indicates the growing concern. A former philosophy professor and Secretary of the Department of Education puts together a collection of moral stories, a book about virtues, for parents to read to their children. The book is a runaway best seller. A national news magazine trumpets the growth of a "politics of virtue" as politicians from both the left and right stress old-fashioned themes of moral character. The nation's president proclaims national "Character Counts" week to promote the "six pillars of character": responsibility, trustworthiness, respect, caring, fairness, and citizenship. On public television Dr. Laura Schlessinger lectures on "Character, Courage, and Conscience." Even in the academic realm, ethics courses return to the classical emphasis on virtue, and books with titles like *Vice and Virtue in Everyday Life* are widely adopted.

In such a contemporary context, we think our book on sportsmanship is important and timely. We can't expect children to do what is right if we don't teach them. We can't expect children to become good people unless we attempt to instill good habits in them and help them develop good character traits. Virtue, said Aristotle, requires practice. We contend that one can, and must, *practice* sportsmanship, just as one must practice a fast break, a base-running situation, or the timing for a poach in tennis doubles. But we can't teach children sportsmanship and guide them in its practice if we don't know what it is or why it's important. While many have bemoaned the situation in today's sports world, there appears to be little available in the way of a clear articulation of the basic principles of sportsmanship.

Given the overwhelming numbers of young people involved in sports as participants, spectators, and fans, it is imperative to reclaim moral language for sport in order for this part of their lives to be charged with the possibilities of moral growth and excellence of character. Sport is not the only arena, but it can and should be an important one for practicing virtue. And it doesn't just happen of its own accord. Sport can—and often does—inculcate the worst habits, the worst character. In 1962 Brutus Hamilton, the great track and field coach, said: "When ideals are obscured in amateur sports, then comes the danger of an athletic injury to the character of the athlete" (Walton,

p. 117). One thing is sure: How we conduct ourselves as players, coaches, parents, and school administrators will make its mark upon the kinds of human beings we are going to be. Sport is an expression of our culture; and because of the enormous importance we attribute to it, it shapes that culture as well.

Being a good sport also requires *proper perspective* about what sporting activity is and what its central values are. In this sense, sportsmanship involves a kind of wisdom that requires proper insight, right attitudes, and good judgment, as well as appropriate conduct. Sport can and should teach lessons, and such lessons can be crucial for self-understanding. As you will see, we believe that sportsmanship primarily involves *respect*—for the opponent, for teammates, for officials, for coaches, and for the game. The principles of good sportsmanship do not supply specific rules for behavior; rather, they supply the general guidelines and the context in which good judgment, relying on experience and understanding, can arrive at specific decisions in a meaningful way. It is precisely that context that seems to be missing in today's sport culture.

The thread that runs through the entire book is a philosophic return to the old-fashioned notion of sportsmanship as the unifying moral concept that describes good character in sport. We choose the word *sportsmanship* as our central concept after much consideration and much discussion with coaches and ex-coaches who care about the sorts of things we are trying to express. As for it being old-fashioned, we need a word that carries the weight of tradition, for it is our contention that we need to get back in touch with something we were once in touch with. We also hasten to say that the second syllable of the word *sportsmanship* should not be taken to exclude female athletes; indeed, it's arguable that girls' and women's athletics has continued to place a far greater emphasis on sportsmanship than the male version. We occasionally resort to the expression "being a good sport," but even that expression doesn't have the resonance of the traditional noun. In an informal survey, we found several women's basketball coaches, themselves women, who quite reasonably avoid the expression "man-to-man" defense but don't hesitate to use the expression "sportsmanship." Our position is simple: Excellence of character, on the playing field and in life generally, is just as important for girls and women as it is for boys and men.

We hope this book will be useful as a basis for discussion and reflection about virtuous conduct in sport. We want this book to engage and provoke you, as well as guide and instruct. Throughout the book we provide questions and examples for further discussion and reflection. Admittedly, we tend to use examples from the sports we are most experienced in, but the general principles of sportsman-like character derive from the nature of sport, not from a specific sport. We hope that you will come up with your own situations and examples from the sports we've devoted less time to—and reflect on them in light of the principles we articulate. We believe that something good happens to people when they engage in dialogue and reflection about important human concerns. Long ago Socrates argued that we should be most concerned about virtue and the greatest possible care of our souls. He exhorted his fellow Athenians to try, above all, to make themselves as good and as wise as possible. Reading a book on sportsmanship and thinking about such issues may appear to be a trivial response to Socrates' challenge. Yet where else do we have such an opportunity to connect with young people in an area they care about and raise these questions again and again? Why not exhort young athletes to be as good and as wise as possible when they play their games, as well as in life as a whole?

Acknowledgments

Many of my colleagues here at Tarleton—in P.E. and athletics, English, Social Sciences, and even administration—offered encouragement and suggestions. It would be impossible to mention them all, but I'd like to single out a few individuals who offered detailed critiques of the early drafts of the manuscript. Reed Richmond, Tarleton's sports information director, offered numerous examples to illustrate the principles we discuss. Larry Bicket filled the manuscript with remarks and suggestions, some of which were actually helpful. My colleague and wife, Mallory Young, as always, was my best reader and critic; and I thank her for suffering through yet another sports obsession.

Other friends were remarkably helpful. Mark Sinnett wrote more on his copy of the manuscript than the copyeditor (no surprise coming from a Presbyterian mathematician-theologian), and we spent a fine afternoon discussing his suggestions. Monty McCutchen read the chapter on respect for officials and helped us gain the kind of perspective that we advocate. His idea that referees are the "reminders of our humanness" was a great capsule statement for that chapter.

The students in my graduate Philosophy of Sport course in the fall of 1996 were enthusiastic guinea pigs, and they helped to come up with questions for our "Time-Outs for Reflection," as well as suggestions for the appendix. Even Barry.

Craig Clifford

First, I am most grateful to my wife Barb, who listened to me, gave me moral support, and even helped with some of the typing. I want to thank the people who read the manuscript in its earliest form and offered encouraging words. Special thanks to Travis and Carol Feezell, both fine coaches, for good conversations about the book and some helpful examples. I also want to acknowledge many helpful conversations with my longtime friend and coaching colleague, Paul Davis. Finally, thanks to Evan for his indirect but important influence.

Randolph M. Feezell

Jointly, we would like to thank Bill Stephens of the Philosophy Department at Creighton for ferrying e-mail messages from the one of us who, technologically speaking, has entered the 20th century to the one who has not.

Finally, we'd like to express appreciation to Jim Kestner and Marni Basic at Human Kinetics. Their professionalism and dedication to the importance of the project were admirable.

Becoming Reflective

An Invitation to Coaches

Whether you are a new coach or a relatively experienced coach, you have probably used the term "sportsmanship" at some time or other. And certainly you've heard others use the term. Perhaps some sportscaster questions the sportsmanship of running up the score to impress the pollsters. Maybe a member of the school board questions the overemphasis on winning and the lack of emphasis on sportsmanship in contemporary sports.

But have you taken the time to think carefully about the issues involved? What is sportsmanship? Why is it important? How important is it? Am I teaching this value to my players? Would I ever be willing to sacrifice winning for the value of sportsmanship? Should I be?

These are difficult questions that every coach must face. Have you taken the time to reflect carefully about them? As a coach you are now one of the most important people in the lives of many young people. You have a responsibility to those who listen to you and who look up to you. As a coach you are supposed to be a teacher, but have you thought about what your players are learning from you besides the fundamentals and strategies of your sport? We often talk about how important role models are for our children. Do you realize that many of your players may see you as a kind of role model? Are you comfortable with this? Does your behavior reflect the kind of person you want your players to be?

In this book we want to help you think about these things, and we'll offer suggestions for how you might apply your insights to your actual coaching. As we have said, these are difficult issues—among the most difficult any coach must face. They involve some perplexing questions, but they are, in some sense, unavoidable. As a coach you must face tough decisions about ethical matters daily, and many of these matters ultimately relate to your most basic views about the very nature of sport—why it's important to you, why you care about it, and how it relates to the other things in your life that matter to you.

While you can scarcely avoid the many situations in which you must make important ethical decisions, you can certainly avoid thoughtfully engaging these issues. This avoidance is what we want to challenge in this book. We want to challenge you to become more reflective about coaching. We want you to think *with* us. You may not agree with everything we say, but that's natural. Our goal is not to preach, but to encourage and to help. We will encourage you to think for yourself, and we'll challenge you to develop your own answers to these questions. We believe, however, that we can help you think about these issues and give you a framework within which you can make your own decisions and help your players grow, not only as athletes but also as human beings. The ultimate goal of ethical reflection is practical: it makes a difference in how you act, how you treat others, and in what kind of person you are.

In part I, "Thinking About Sportsmanship," we'll provide a foundation for the rest of the book. In part II, "The Principles of Sportsmanship," we'll develop a series of principles derived from the foundation we've laid down in part I. These are the principles that we hope you'll apply to your coaching. In part III, "Thinking About Sport and Life," we'll ask you to go beyond the playing fields of athletic competition and think about the relationship between sport and the rest of life. Finally, in the appendix we'll offer some concrete suggestions for how you might go about teaching the principles of sportsmanship to young athletes.

Some of the things we'll say in part I might seem somewhat abstract, but the principles of sportsmanship that we'll offer in part II—respect for opponents, for the team, for officials, for the game—must be based on *something*. Otherwise, they will float about as nothing more than groundless recommendations. We believe these principles of respect are not merely our subjective impressions. Ultimately, the principles of sportsmanship are grounded in the very nature of what we're about as players, coaches, and human beings. Thinking about sport, as we'll see in part III, will inevitably lead us to the most fundamental questions about life. So bear with us—and think with us. The beautiful jump shot you had in high school won't help you, but the tenacity and courage that you've developed in the heat of athletic competition will.

PART ONE

Thinking About Sportsmanship

CHAPTER 1

Reflecting on Your Own Experience

© CLEO Photography

> The unexamined life is not worth living.
>
> —Plato, *Apology of Socrates*

The best place to start this process is with your own experience. We will ask you to allow your own experience—and your understanding of it—to be challenged, but we won't ask you to leave that experience behind. Most of you probably already attempt to instill the values of sportsmanship in your players. But how important is it in your coaching? Do your players exhibit sportsmanlike behavior? Do you?

A CHALLENGE TO REFLECT

Here are some questions that might help you reflect on your own experience. Write out your answers.

1. Who are the coaches I most respect? Why do I respect them? What qualities do they have that I most admire?
2. How do I want to be remembered by my athletes? How will they think of me later in life? Will I have made some difference in their lives? Will they want their children to play for me?
3. Am I the kind of coach I would want my children to play for? If not, why?
4. Which of my former coaches do I most admire? Which of my former coaches do I least admire? Why?
5. Do I care most about being liked or being respected by my players? Do my players like me? Respect me? Neither? Both?

What do your answers show you about your own coaching? What do they indicate about how serious you are about sportsmanship and character? These questions are meant to challenge you to look squarely at your own sense of what really matters to you as a coach.

RESPECT STARTS WITH YOU

Here are the personal reflections of one current coach about his own past experience:

My American Legion baseball coach was one of the finest persons I've ever met. He never raised his voice. He was gentle but firm. I never saw him argue with an umpire. He treated every player with the utmost respect. He made us practice long and hard, but my impression was that all the players felt grateful to be coached by him. We all tried as hard as we could—for him.

If you messed up, especially if you made a mental error, one little glance from him was enough to make you realize how much you had let him and the team down. He never allowed us to yell at other players or rag the umpires. And other coaches and teams knew this. I saw umpires apologize to him for making bad calls. He taught us the values of respect, responsibility, team play, and effort. It's really hard to put into words what he meant to all of us. I would have tried to run through a brick wall for him, and I know I'm a better person because I played for him.

Maybe we can't all be revered like this coach, but examples from your own experience probably show how much coaches can matter to players. Don't underestimate the extent to which players make judgments about their coaches. Because of your behavior, your players know that you approve of some things and disapprove of others. They know that you have certain values. What values are you conveying to your players? Answer the following questions honestly.

1. Do you allow your players to "talk trash" to opponents?
2. Do you allow your players to respond to an officiating call with angry displays of temper?
3. Do you let your players "showboat," or prance, after they do something positive?
4. Do you ever yell or scream at players?
5. If you do yell or scream at players, do you do it when they perform poorly or when they behave in an unsportsmanlike manner?
6. Would you allow your team to depart after a game without shaking the opponents' hands?
7. Have you ever blamed a loss on an official (especially when talking to your players after the game)?
8. Have you ever made excuses for losing a game?
9. Would you attempt to intimidate an official in order to get a favorable call in the future?
10. Would you get into a heated argument with an official in order to motivate your team?
11. Would you promote animosity between two teammates to motivate them?
12. Would you run up the score on a team for any reason?
13. Do you ever call your players names in a way that demeans them or publicly embarrasses them?
14. Do you treat your players differently after a loss than after a win?

15. Do you punish or reward your players as a result of whether the team won or lost a match or game, without regard for the effort they put out?

THINKING ABOUT REASONS

Now take another step. Go back through the questions we just asked and ask yourself *why* you do or don't engage in these practices. If, for example, you do allow your players to talk trash to opponents, why? If you don't, why don't you? If you would run up the score on an opponent, why? If not, why not? And so on. Do you have good reasons for your answers? In other words, ask yourself not just what you *do* in your coaching, but what you think you *should* be doing. Go back through each of the questions and ask yourself, regardless of what you actually do, whether you condone or condemn the practice. And then ask yourself what reasons you have for each judgment.

If you're willing to reflect on the reasons behind your actions and attitudes—which means that you're willing to risk the possibility of admitting you're wrong if your reasons don't hold up—then we think you'll find the following chapters helpful. We won't tell you exactly how you ought to answer these questions. We will, however, articulate a set of principles in light of which you ought to address these questions. These principles may challenge the way you've answered them—at the very least this should be an opportunity to become more reflective about what you do. Or you may very well come away from this book with the same answers to these questions, but with a better understanding of the reasons behind your answers—and your actions.

COMMON OBJECTIONS TO TEACHING SPORTSMANSHIP

We can imagine that some coaches might be skeptical about our emphasis on sportsmanship and "coaching for character." It's not universally agreed that coaches have a responsibility to teach sportsmanship. Some of the objections are fairly prevalent, and we'd like to respond to them before we get underway. We'll let "Coach Skeptical," a hypothetical character who will appear from time to time throughout the book, state the objections.

Coach Skeptical: Times have changed. Players and coaches act differently than they did in the past. Other successful coaches let their players trash talk or vent their emotions, so why shouldn't I? You just can't expect players to act like monks or nuns. Why can't coaches let players be themselves?

Times may have changed, but in a very important sense, the sports we coach and play have not. Just because more people today, in sport and in society at large, act in disrespectful and uncivil ways doesn't mean that we must judge such actions as acceptable. Instead of throwing up our hands and saying kids are different so we must coach them differently, we should ask ourselves whether in fact they are different because we've coached them—and in general educated them—differently. It may be that because there is such an emphasis on winning and being "Number One" we have forgotten the extent to which the language of sportsmanship has been central to the great athletic traditions. If unsportsmanlike behavior now seems to be the status quo, that doesn't mean that it has to be. It does mean that coaches have a huge responsibility to constantly teach, practice, and exemplify good sportsmanship. Someone must step forward and challenge the status quo. The truth of the matter is, sportsmanship doesn't restrict self-expression or require monkish behavior. There are good reasons for requiring players to be good sports, and people with good moral character are no less free to "express" themselves than are bad sports. They may simply do this differently.

Coach Skeptical: I'm paid to coach, not to be a parent, baby-sitter, or "moral educator," whatever that means. My job is to coach, not teach values. That's a job for families and churches, not coaches. If kids are less respectful nowadays, that's not my fault. I have to work with the hand I've been dealt.

You don't have any choice. You're a role model and a moral educator, whether you like it or not. The issue is not whether you, as a coach, choose to convey values; the issue is whether you choose to convey the values of *sportsmanship* and whether you make this teaching a conscious part of your coaching. Would you want your child to play for a coach who wants no part of teaching values? Wouldn't you want your child to be taught to respect others, love the game, be responsible, trustworthy, fair?

Coach Skeptical: Sports are about winning and losing. You don't learn lessons by losing. Winning is the point—period. That's what we should be teaching our children. Life is competitive. If you want to get ahead, you'd better be realistic about these things. Sports teach you to hate losing, to love winning, and to do whatever is necessary in order to win. If I have to intimidate opponents or officials to win, so be it. And if others don't, that's their problem. I'll win, and they'll lose. Sports teach you to make the other guy the loser.

First of all, in many, if not most, cases it's a mistake to think that teaching and requiring good sportsmanship from your players is inconsistent with the pursuit of victory. In fact, as we'll argue, not taking the pursuit of victory seriously is unsportsmanlike. There have been and continue to be fine coaches who demand both athletic excellence and moral excellence from their players. John Wooden is merely one example of a successful coach who insisted on character and integrity.

But, more importantly, the view that winning at all costs is what matters is based on a misunderstanding of sport and competition. In an interview for a *60 Minutes* segment on sportsmanship, Kareem Abdul-Jabbar, whose ability to win certainly wasn't stifled by John Wooden's emphasis on sportsmanship, remarked:

> *Our whole culture here in America has become a lot more vulgar. And I think it's not considered cool to be a good sportsman. You're considered square and soft. . . .There's the whole process of celebration that's gone beyond celebration. It's taunting. I pity the people who are doing this, because they really don't understand: Sports is a step away from the rule of the jungle, and they're trying to move it back towards the jungle, when the strong survive and misuse the weaker in any way that they want. And that's really unfortunate for our whole system of values in our country.*

WRAP-UP

As we'll argue in chapter 2, teaching sportsmanship is not a matter of imposing standards of behavior that come from outside the arena of sport. What Kareem reminds us is that unsportsmanlike conduct is the result of misunderstanding the nature of sport. Unsportsmanlike conduct is conduct that is contrary to the nature of sport, and sportsmanlike conduct is conduct that is consistent with the nature of sport. Bad sportsmanship, then, is at least in part the result of bad understanding. To understand why Kareem would say that sport is a step away from the law of the jungle, we'll have to spend some time—pardon the sports metaphor—in the weight room and on the practice field of thinking. We'll have to think about the nature of sport. In this chapter you have begun the process of thinking about these difficult and important issues. But, mostly, we have challenged you with questions that have forced you to reflect on your own experience as a coach. Now we want to help you think, not just about your personal experience, but about the nature of the activity you're engaged in.

CHAPTER 2

Sportsmanship and the Nature of Sport

© Daily Illini

> Neither are the two arts of music and gymnastic really designed, as is often supposed, the one for the training of the soul, the other for the training of the body.
>
> What then is the real object of them?
>
> I believe, I said, that the teachers of both have in view chiefly the improvement of the soul.
>
> —Plato, *Republic (Jowett translation)*
>
> The true athlete should have good character, not be a character.
>
> —John Wooden

In this chapter, we want you to think hard about the very nature of the activity in which you are involved. Perhaps you've never asked yourself, in an explicit way, the most basic question: What is sport? But as we have already suggested, there's little doubt that your approach to coaching probably assumes some answer to this question. In this chapter we'll ask you to make your assumptions explicit—and to examine them. We'll ask you to think explicitly about the nature of sport. At various points, we'll stop and imagine how some coaches might respond to what we're saying. So imagine that you're engaged in a conversation with us. At other times, we'll take a brief time-out to enable you to reflect on the issue that we're raising.

WHY SPORTSMANSHIP?

Why sportsmanship? Actually, as Kareem's remarks in chapter 1 reminded us, the first question is: Why sport? It's impossible to say why sportsmanship is important—or even what it is—without some understanding of what sport is all about. Why do we play these games? Why do we encourage our children to play them? Why do we include sports in our schools?

Some educators have questioned the value of the competitive experience in an educational setting, on the playing field as well as in the classroom, while others insist that participation in sports is a valuable experience, even a necessary educational experience. Detractors say the competitive situation is debilitating, that it instills bad character traits, that "cooperative learning" ought to displace competitive learning; defenders say that "sport builds character," that competition provides a unique opportunity for learning.

Some of these disagreements run deep, and they ultimately have to do with profoundly different views of what life is all about; but on both sides there's a good deal of confusion about the *nature* of the activity. Why sportsmanship? Why sport? How we answer those questions depends on how we answer another question: What is sport? In other words, what is the *nature* of sport?

Of course, this question has generated volumes of learned reflection by anthropologists, sociologists, psychologists, and philosophers. We certainly can't fully address this question here, but it is possible to offer a brief sketch of an answer.

Coach Skeptical: Come on, guys, the "nature" of sport? We all know what sport is. The only question is how to be good at it.

We all operate with some idea—well, it might be an assumption— about the nature of sport. We're saying that it's something we need to consciously think about.

Coach Skeptical: I need to think about how to get my players motivated to win. Thinking about the nature of sport isn't going to help me do that.

Suppose you think that sport is something we do to escape from the drudgery of work—a kind of pleasant release from the things that really matter. That it's "fun." It's "play." And that its purpose is to help us relax so that we can go back to work, which is what really matters, refreshed. Wouldn't that have an effect on how you would treat your players? Run a practice? Coach a game?

Or say you think that sport is an arena for the strong to triumph over the weak, winners over losers. That it's about winning, and only about winning. Would that view of the nature of sport have an effect on the way you approached coaching?

Of course it would. That's why we're asking you to take a step back from the day-to-day pressures of running a practice, preparing for the arch rival, dealing with irate parents, and talking to the local radio sportscaster. We're asking you to think about what sort of activity you're involved in, because the ideas and assumptions that you carry into coaching have a profound effect on the young people you coach.

THE NATURE OF SPORT

The language we use to talk about sport is revealing. We "play the game," "play ball," "make the play." We call the participants "players." *Sport is a form of play.* Inherent in the idea of play is that, unlike work, we don't have to do it. We freely choose to play. And it's important to note that we freely choose to play, not because playing results in something else that is valuable (although it may), but because we enjoy playing. We play because it's fun, exhilarating, beautiful. In philosophical terms, we play because we find the activity of playing *inherently valuable.* That's why the anthropologist Johan Huizinga refers to the human species as *homo ludens,* "playing man." Far from being a mere escape from "real life," play is a part of who we are.

Of course, there are other forms of play that aren't sport. Kids horsing around on a jungle gym or simply running around the neighborhood burning up energy is play, but it isn't sport. When parents say to a child "Go outside and play," they aren't usually thinking about sport. What, then, distinguishes sport from other forms of play? While sport is still play, there is an element of seriousness about it. Although we sometimes use the term "sport" to refer to noncompetitive physical activities such as fishing or horseback riding for pleasure, in the context of school or club athletics, sport takes on this air of seriousness because it involves competition—and because this competition is governed by rules and customs. The rules spell out the nature of the competition, and they establish the boundaries of fairness within which winning is meaningful. But competition does involve winning and losing. Players "play" the game, but they pit their skills and abilities against the skills of opponents, and even against other participants, past, present, and future. Within the context of the game, one player is *better* than another; one team is *better* than another. Because the kind of sport we're concerned with here is competitive, better and worse matter. It's play, but it's serious; it's fun, but it's difficult; it can be exhilarating, but it can be heartbreaking.

Sport, then, is a form of play, a competitive, rule-governed activity that human beings freely choose to engage in. Understanding this, we must play it as if it is absolutely important while never forgetting that it's a form of play that, in a certain sense, doesn't really matter. Ultimately, the principles of sportsmanship are based on the delicate balance of playfulness and seriousness that is at the heart of sport.

TIME-OUT *for Reflection*

- Which do you emphasize more: the seriousness or the playfulness of competition? If you think in terms of a scale from total playfulness to total seriousness, where do you place yourself on the scale?

- What do you say in practice or during and after a game to remind your players that sport is a form of play? What are some of the common expressions that draw attention to the playful character of sport?

- What do you say to draw attention to the serious side of sport? To its competitive nature? What are some of the common expressions that draw attention to the seriousness of competition?

- Suppose your team has just lost a well-fought game against a superior opponent. How often do you do the following:

  –Say something like "It's only a game" or "Your mother will still love you"?

  –Blow up and tell them they didn't "want it bad enough"?

  –Commend them for their play and their behavior?

  –Commend the opponents for their play and behavior?

  –Punish the team for losing (with an extra practice, extra running, or the like)?

THREE PERSPECTIVES ON COMPETITION: FINDING THE MIDDLE WAY

When we forget the balance of playfulness and seriousness, sportsmanship falls by the wayside. Two extreme views of competition are based on a confusion about the balance of playfulness and seriousness in sport. Our intention is to offer a middle way that preserves this essential balance.

At one extreme is the view that winning is everything and the only thing, that nothing is ever gained in losing, except learning that losing is bad. Competition on this model is like war: The opponent is the enemy and the goal is to destroy the enemy. At the other extreme is the view that competition is inherently bad, that all forms of play in which there are winners and losers are unethical, psychologically destructive, educationally ineffective. On this view, only noncompetitive play is acceptable. Sports are acceptable only if they are organized, coached, and taught in such a way that winning—and therefore talent and ability—doesn't matter at all. On this view, "having fun" is the only thing that matters.

The winning-is-everything approach loses track of the spirit of play; the fun-is-everything approach loses track of the seriousness. To the one, we ought to say "Lighten up" and to the other, "Get serious." From the standpoint of the middle ground on which sport is both playful and serious, both of these extremes are based on the same misunderstanding of the nature of competition.

On one level, competition does involve winners and losers; and, more specifically, if one side wins, the other necessarily loses. But on another level, competition is an opportunity for the development, exercise, and expression of human excellence. Trying to win means trying to do the best I can at the game, trying to be as excellent as possible in all of the ways that the game calls for. But it is precisely my opponent's effort to excel, my opponent's effort to perform better than I do, that gives me the opportunity to strive for excellence. By the same token, I make it possible for my opponent to strive for excellence. In that sense I ought to be thankful for a great opponent. On one level opponents "oppose" each other; on another level they are engaged in a *mutual striving for excellence.*[1] If it's valuable to play, then my opponent is valuable to me; without an opponent I can't play. On the playing field, "cooperative" and "competitive" learning are not opposites, for good competition is cooperation.

Of course, it's little wonder that some people would conclude that competition is inherently bad if their competitive experiences have been characterized by the winning-is-everything attitude. If winning is everything and you're better than I am, then what's the point? If I'm going to lose, it's pretty obvious that my only rational choice is to refuse to compete. Or, if I am better than you and you will get nothing from losing to me, then my beating you is nothing short of exploitation. Both of those situations would be morally repugnant.

At the other extreme, if you teach kids that winning doesn't matter at all, you're not being honest about the nature of competition. If it doesn't matter at all whether I win or lose, if it doesn't matter at all whether I throw the ball well or poorly, what's the point? If the winning-is-everything extreme is morally repugnant, the winning-is-nothing extreme is morally inane. A beginning youth league might well employ a rule that all players play a certain number of minutes to allow all of the participants an opportunity to learn the skills of the

---

[1] We take the phrase "mutual striving" from Drew Hyland, "Competition and Friendship," *Journal of the Philosophy of Sport* V (1978). Hyland points out that the word "competition" derives from the Latin *com-petitio,* meaning "to question or strive together."

game, but such a rule employed to downplay the competitive aspect of the game misses the point of competition.

To steer a course between these extremes, we have to articulate the value of *participating* in the game and the opportunity that that participation affords. At the risk of combating clichés with clichés, we do need to return to the notion that, at some deeper level, it's not whether you win or lose—after all, somebody must lose for somebody else to win—but how you play the game. In fact, we can take this idea one step further: It's not just how *you* play the game that ultimately matters, but how the *game* is played, for it is participation in that game that is valuable. How I play the game contributes to the quality of that game for me, my teammates, coach, and opponents—even spectators and the community.

It's not whether you win or lose, but what kind of game everyone gets to participate in. Central to the game is the effort of the participants to win, and without the participants' commitment to winning, there is no game. It is not, however, the winning itself that ultimately matters, but the sorts of things we experience and come to understand by playing the game and the opportunities for human excellence that playing the game affords.

Coach Skeptical: But if you tell your players that winning isn't everything, will they try as hard to win? Will it matter enough to them? I want my players to be as competitive as they can be. I want them to hurt like I do when they lose. Isn't it still winning that really matters?

Don't misunderstand what we're saying. We believe that winning really matters—and that it should matter. But it matters within the context of participating in an exhilarating experience of trying to become excellent, and learning things about ourselves. The main problem with the winning-is-everything attitude is that it diminishes the importance of all the other good things about sport. It's like going to a good movie and saying the only good thing about it was how it turned out. An understanding of the richness of sport helps us sustain the balance of playfulness and seriousness, and this very balance provides space for other important values—including sportsmanship—to flourish. In fact, what we're saying is that competitiveness—striving to win—is an essential part of sportsmanship.

SPORT AND VIRTUE

One of the assumptions we make in this book is that coaches—and, for that matter, administrators, parents, fans, officials, and everyone else involved in youth athletics—are moral educators, whether they want to be or not. That does not mean that they are moral indoctrinators—indeed, they should not indoctrinate. It does mean, however, that, inescapably, they play a role in the formation of character.

For this reason, it is important to understand that sportsmanship is not just a matter of acceptable behavior but of *excellence of character*—or, in the language of the classical tradition—*sportsmanship is a virtue*. It is not altogether coincidental that there has been a return to the classical understanding of virtue right at a time when so many of our athletic superstars in professional and big-time college sports have become models of anything and everything but good character. It is particularly sad, because sport has long provided an arena in which the central ethical concept has been excellence of character. Part of the purpose of this book is to reclaim the moral language that was—and to a large extent still is—part of the great athletic traditions harkening all the way back to the Olympian ideals that we continue to celebrate every four years as well as the language of classical ethical thought that harkens all the way back to ancient Greek philosophy.

There are some pitfalls to this language. The English word "virtue," in certain contexts, has the connotation of moral purity, of having avoided the stain of vice. In that context, one is virtuous by *not* doing something. We mean by "virtue" not moral purity but *excellence of character*.[2] When we speak of a return to a "virtue-centered ethics," we have in mind the turn from ethics centered on principles and rules for right action and good conduct to ethics centered on the importance of good character. Sportsmanship, then, is not just about following rules, behaving a certain way because that's the way you're supposed to behave; it's about what sort of human beings we choose to become. When William Bennett, former Secretary of Education, put out *The Book of Virtues* in 1993, a good part of what he had in mind was the classical notion of virtue as excellence of character. His notion is that stories can provide models of excellent character. Our notion—and, of course, it's not our notion, but a very old one—is that athletic competition can provide an arena for the *practice* of virtue, that is, for development of excellent character.

Because virtue is at least in part a matter of deeply ingrained habits, it makes sense to say that a person can practice virtue. If I lack self-discipline, I need opportunities—not overwhelmingly difficult ones to begin with—to develop the habit of self-discipline. If I lack courage and self-confidence, I need the opportunity to develop courage and

---

[2]Both "virtue" and "excellence" have been used as translations of the classical Greek *aretē*, the central concept in Plato's and Aristotle's ethical thought.

self-confidence. Likewise, if sportsmanship is a virtue, it makes sense to say that one can practice sportsmanship. It is essential to recognize that all the principles or rules for behavior that we'll articulate in the following chapters are grounded in the notion that they develop excellence of character.

There may be a good deal of disagreement about exactly how to flesh out the content of an excellent character. It would be impossible here to attempt to list and think through even the most historically important recommendations concerning the central human virtues: wisdom, courage, self-control, justice, honesty, autonomy, humility, benevolence, love, authenticity, compassion, responsibility, respectfulness . . . the list would be quite long. What is clear, though, is that sport requires and shapes character traits. It's not by any means the only arena—so is the classroom, the music practice room, and, in most households, the room with the biggest TV set—but it's an important one. How you set up a practice, talk about the game, respond to discipline problems—everything you do—sets the tone, takes a stand on what sort of character traits you value. How you respond to a lazy player who merely goes through the motions of a strenuous drill, a player's taunting of an opponent, a player of mediocre talent whose effort was superb—all of these responses tell young athletes what kind of character you value, what sort of human beings they should aspire to be. In short, we're better off to admit that we are moral educators, try to think as clearly about these difficult issues as we can, and develop our athletic programs accordingly. Coaches don't simply stamp out human character like, say, automobiles in a factory. In fact, one of the things we have to remember is that coaches have to make good judgments, not only about the abilities and limits of athletic ability but also about the natural dispositions and limitations of character. But coaches do provide an opportunity for the practice of virtue.

In fleshing out the virtue of sportsmanship, you'll come to see that practicing sportsmanship means practicing an attitude of respect. Respect is an attitude of positive evaluation, a recognition of something, some reality that merits understanding and attentiveness. To respect something is to value it and treat it as worthy in its own right. To respect something I have to overcome my inclination to be selfish, my inclination to see the thing only in terms of my own needs and interests. To respect my parents or to respect my country, for example, is to esteem or to honor something outside myself, and to realize that there are right and wrong ways to act in relation to these independent realities.

To be a good sport I must understand my situation and see things broadly, not simply in terms of self-centered desires to win, to be famous, or to be mentioned in the headlines of the local newspaper. As a player or participant I should respect opponents, teammates, officials, the coach, and, in the broadest sense, the very activity in which I am engaged. It is important to remember, however, that we are talking not simply about rules for behavior, but about the *habit of respect*—a habit of respect that becomes a part of someone's character.

TIME-OUT *for Reflection*

- How often do the following words or expressions come out of your mouth?

  –Character

  –Integrity

  –Class, class act

  –Dignity

  –Respect

  –Sportsmanship

  –Honor

  –Humility

- The list of cardinal virtues for classical Greek civilization included wisdom, self-control, courage, and justice. What kinds of situations call for these cardinal virtues?

- Come up with your own list of virtues. If you believe that sport builds character, what are the character traits, the virtues, that you think sport builds?

- Put into your own words what it means to have an attitude of respect. Do you think that young people today are less inclined to exhibit this attitude? If so, why has this come about?

SPORT, GOOD JUDGMENT, AND SELF-UNDERSTANDING

As a moral educator you have to make good judgments yourself; but it bears mentioning that you are also providing the arena in which your players can develop good judgment. We may be able to say in a general way what sportsmanship is—and you may be able to explain it to your players—but that doesn't mean we can tell you exactly what the sportsmanlike thing to do will be in every particular situation. And you will not be able to tell your players in every situation how to apply these principles. The practice and development of good character, as well as its exercise, requires good judgment. As we articulate the principles of good sportsmanship in the chapters that follow, the first thing that will come to mind for anyone with athletic experience is that it's often difficult to determine in a particular situation what is the appropriate way to exercise respect for opponents (chapter 3), respect for teammates (chapter 4), respect for officials (chapter 5), respect for the game (chapter 6), or respect between players and coaches (chapter 7). If an opponent repeatedly demonstrates disrespect for me and for the game, for example, how do I respond in such a way as to demonstrate that I understand my need for a good opponent and my respect for the game? We will provide examples of difficult situations, and we encourage you to think them through, discuss them, and try to figure out how to respond in light of the principles of sportsmanship that we articulate here. We hasten to point out that the difficulty that some situations present for the realization of these principles doesn't mean that the principles are invalid. Many situations and many actions and responses by athletes are clear as day, and we'll provide examples of that nature as well. In that sense, good stories about heroes and villains are essential. Indeed, the fact that decisions in light of principles are sometimes difficult doesn't mean that we should abandon principles. It is precisely when the situations are difficult that we need to stress deliberation in light of principles.

One of the dangers of a simplistic approach to the idea that sport builds character is that we can forget the essential role of deliberation and judgment and understanding, especially of self-understanding. Sport handled well provides an opportunity to understand the importance of truthfulness about oneself and about one's relationships to others. Self-understanding has largely to do with coming to terms with limits—understanding what I *can* do and what I *can't* do. Ultimately, all true possibility comes from understanding limits, for knowing the limits of what I am capable of means knowing what I am capable of. In an athletic contest, that kind of understanding is essential, from both the technical standpoint of trying to figure out how to beat an opponent and the moral standpoint of trying to figure out what sort of person I am capable of being. I have to know my own strengths and weaknesses to compete well. If I'm a gymnast like Dominique Dawes, I want to develop a floor exercise routine that takes advantage of my explosive athleticism; if I'm more like Shannon

Miller I want to emphasize precision, control, and grace. If I'm a baseball player with no power but good speed, I need to develop my skills as a slap hitter and I'd better be able to lay down a good bunt. If I'm an archer with a tendency to get complacent after shooting three or four good ends, I need to admit that I have this weakness. I might need to develop the habit of telling myself, no matter how good the last end was, that I could shoot a few points higher if I would only bear down harder.

Of course, self-understanding of limits includes the recognition of *apparent* limits, which can lead to one of the most rewarding athletic experiences—overcoming apparent limits. Sometimes young athletes (and old ones) think they are capable of much more than they are; and sometimes they are capable of more—sometimes much more—than they think they are. Knowing which is which is not easy, but it's central to the athletic experience. To bombard young athletes with the fiction that anything is possible if they work hard enough, want it bad enough, or visualize it long enough may sometimes be effective locker-room rhetoric; but the truth can be effective, too. Why not say to a young athlete, when the occasion calls for it, "I'm not going to tell you that anything is possible, because it isn't; but I do think you are capable of much more than you realize"?

Of course, if winning is everything, then there is no room for self-understanding about limits. If winning is everything, then anything is possible. If we lost the game, then we should have done something else to win. But there's a difference between reasonably exhorting young athletes to do more than they think they are capable of and pushing them to cheat, to use steroids, or to psychologically self-destruct. There's a difference, for example, between demanding fitness of a young female gymnast within the limits of her growing body and driving her to anorexic eating habits that will carry over into the rest of her life.

Sportsmanship requires an understanding that all of us are finite human beings with finite strengths, that we are all limited; but at the same time it requires that we understand how athletic competition gives us an opportunity to *excel*, to develop ourselves and in a certain sense to transcend ourselves, to become better. The word "sportsmanship" is shorthand for a whole complex of character traits that athletic competition should instill in our young people; but inextricably bound up with the development of that character is the judgment and the understanding—*seeing the way things are*—that make it possible to exercise that character.

And, perhaps even more importantly, because athletic competition always involves understanding ourselves in relation to others, it provides an arena for the development of judgment about human relations. I must not only know my own strengths and weaknesses, but my strengths and weaknesses in relation to my opponents' or to my teammates'. I have to pit my abilities against an opponent's in such a way as to gain a relative advantage—and usually that doesn't mean I get the opportunity simply to pit my strength against his or her weakness. My crosscourt forehand may be my strongest shot, but my opponent's may be stronger; even though I'd rather hit my forehand, I may realize that backhand rallies will give me the edge. And, as I seek the advantage that might allow me to win, I have to keep sight of the deeper level at which our competition binds us together. I can come to understand and respect the efforts of others, and I can come to respect and admire the achievements and talents of others. In a team sport, I have to fit my abilities into the web of interrelations that makes up a team. If, for example, I shoot a basketball like I was born with boxing gloves on, I need to set picks for my teammates who can shoot. I have to understand the mystery of the whole becoming greater than the sum of the parts, that, when the team clicks, the individual participants get back more than they put into it.

TIME-OUT *for Reflection*

- Apply these reflections about limits and apparent limits to yourself. What are the weaknesses that you need to be aware of? Strengths? Think not just in terms of your technical prowess as a coach, but in terms of moral character.

- There's a saying that "Your greatest strength is your greatest weakness." What does that mean?

- What do you do and say to your players to help them understand their own limits, their own strengths and weaknesses as athletes and as human beings?

- What do you do and say to your players to help them overcome apparent limits?

- Rate yourself on a scale from an overwillingness to accept limits at one extreme to the belief that there are no limits at the other. Remember that we're talking here not about locker-room rhetoric, but about understanding the way things are.

- One of the tag lines in Nike's ad campaign during the Centennial Olympic Games was: "You don't win silver, you lose gold." What are the implications of that sentiment?

SPORT, HUMILITY, AND WISDOM

Athletic achievement is a matter of hard work, determination, practice; but it's also a matter of talent and circumstance, of streaks and inexplicable chemistry and magic moments. Even in a culture that often encourages unabashed self-congratulation and self-adulation, many of our greatest athletes react to their achievements with gestures and remarks of thankfulness, humility, even of a kind of reverence: Bjorn Borg falling to his knees at Wimbledon, Dan Jansen's graceful humility after winning an Olympic gold medal in speed skating, Roger Maris so humbled by hitting his 61st home run that his teammates had to physically shove him back out of the dugout so the fans could cheer him. Some athletes express this experience in religious terms, "thanking God for the opportunity." Whether we understand this experience in religious terms or not, in part we do experience—and we should experience—great talent, a great game or series, a great hitting or shooting streak, the chemistry of a great team, as a "gift," an opportunity that is "given" to us.

Great talents can be squandered or developed; but, in the end, talent is something a person is lucky enough to have, not something that he or she earns. (And, as the behavior of some of the most talented individuals all too clearly reveals, we shouldn't infer from the presence of talent that its possessor deserves to possess it.) Almost paradoxically, the experience of great talent, if we think about it honestly, is an occasion for humility and thankfulness. Hakeem Olajuwon may have worked very hard at what he does so well, but how many seven-footers are born with the foot speed of a sprinter and the quickness of a cutting horse? His talent is a thing of beauty: It's something for us to admire and for him to be proud of, but at the same time it's something for him—and for us—to be thankful for.

One of the consequences of understanding talent as a gift is the recognition that talent carries with it special responsibilities. In the movie *Hoosiers*, when the new basketball coach tells the most talented young athlete in town that he has a gift, he is at the same time exhorting him to develop it, to come to deserve it, to let it contribute. As a rule, the greater the talent, the greater the responsibility. Although sport provides one of the few arenas in which we can openly talk about natural ability, it's worth noting here that this rule is not restricted to the playing field.

Along the same lines, great athletic events and achievements are often experienced as opportunities for which the participants and spectators feel grateful. Ask a great hitter in the middle of a streak (or, maybe better, after it's over) how he experiences his accomplishment.

Years of practice and effort are the prerequisites for a streak, and yet, like a slump, there is a sense in which *it just happens*. And there is a sense in which it can't be forced. Good coaches know the expression (and the right moments to use it) "Let it happen." In *Zen in the Art of Archery*, the German philosopher Eugen Herrigel recounts the six years he spent studying archery with a Zen master in Japan. The discipline and dedication and effort are monumental, but the master tells him that the goal of all this hard work is to get to the point at which "it" will shoot the arrows, not him. The Taoists call this *wu-wei*, letting things happen spontaneously and naturally. After winning the men's individual gold medal in archery in the 1996 Summer Olympics, Justin Huish, a 21-year-old Californian, remarked: "I was in a fog, just trying to see gold in my sight and let it rip."

In *Life on the Run* Bill Bradley describes his love of basketball this way:

> *The money and the championships are reasons I play, but what I'm addicted to are the nights like tonight when something special happens on the court. The experience is one of beautiful isolation. It cannot be deduced from the self-evident, like a philosophical proposition. It cannot be generally agreed upon, like an empirically verifiable fact, and it is far more than a passing emotion. It is as if a lightning bolt strikes, brings insight into an uncharted area of human experience. (pp. 220-221)*

In *A River Runs Through It* Norman Maclean describes the art of casting a fly rod in terms of this same mysterious combination of determined hard work and the humility to let it happen:

> *My father was very sure about certain matters pertaining to the universe. To him, all good things—trout as well as eternal salvation—come by grace and grace comes from art and art does not come easy. (p. 4)*

No work, no grace. But, by the same token, work alone cannot achieve it; it cannot be forced. Maclean puts it this way:

> *Well, until man is redeemed he will always take a fly rod too far back, just as natural man always overswings with an ax or golf club and loses all his power somewhere in the air; only with a rod it's worse, because the fly often comes so far back it gets caught behind in a bush or rock. (p. 3)*

The son of a Presbyterian minister, Maclean chooses to call it "grace"; the Zen master says "it" shoots the arrow, that the release of the arrow is like the snow falling from the end of a bamboo leaf. In American sports lingo, we talk about athletes being "in the zone," "on fire," "shooting lights out," "unconscious." It's that experience of being present when something wonderful happens. We come to appreciate how much great moments in sport are a gift for which we should be grateful because we've all been in the situation of saying "It just didn't happen for me today," "I just didn't have it today," or "I tried my best, but it wasn't in the cards. . . ." When it does happen for us, it's wise to feel proud of our achievement, but at the same time lucky to be there.

In that sense, the athletic experience goes beyond the development of character and the calculative understanding of one's strengths and weaknesses; it is an opportunity for a kind of wisdom. Although we may not go so far as to endorse the total selflessness of Zen Buddhism, we can say that sport sometimes does provide an experience of a kind of spirituality that transcends the arrogant egoism that characterizes so much of our culture. The experience in sport of great moments and great talent, far from encouraging the arrogant egoism that we see too often on our TVs, is an occasion for a kind of selfless humility. And that experience of selfless humility can be mysteriously enriching.

We can agree with the Zen master that this is the same spirituality that humans have sought in all the activities that can be done either well or poorly, all of the activities that require dedication, hard work, and grace. In giving yourself over to the activity, something happens to you. Great musicians, like great athletes, give themselves over to the music, and the music comes over them. The same could be said of great writers, dancers, cooks, carpenters, and a host of others. By giving themselves over to something, by giving themselves up to the activity, they are enlarged by it.

TIME-OUT *for Reflection*

- What do you do or say to call attention to those aspects of sport that we can't control, to the things that simply happen but can't be made to happen?

- Do you ever refer to talent as a gift?

- Do you use the word "humility"? Do you think of humility as a virtue?

- Do you think that greater talent implies greater responsibility?

- When you talk to your players after a great game or season, which do you tend to emphasize: that they should be proud of their accomplishment or thankful for the opportunity?

WRAP-UP

Why sportsmanship? Because the nature of sport requires it. Sport understood as rule-governed competitive athletic play requires—and therefore can teach—certain character traits. Without sportsmanship, sport is no longer sport, the game is no longer a game. If the game is valuable—if we play the game for its joy, for its educational value, for its intrinsic beauty, for the truth about ourselves that it opens up— then sportsmanship is indispensable.

Why sportsmanship? Because it matters what sort of human beings we are—and what sort of human beings our children become. Because it's better for human beings to be courageous, disciplined, fair, honest, responsible, humble, and wise than not to be. The complex of character traits that we refer to as the virtue of sportsmanship is "useful"— good character helps us to win games, run a business, develop friendships—but we should be careful not to reduce sportsmanship to a mere expediency. Why sportsmanship? Because good character is good for its own sake, whether we are "rewarded" for it or not. Or, in traditional ethical terms, sportsmanship is its own reward.

PART TWO

The Principles of Sportsmanship

CHAPTER 3

Respect for Opponents

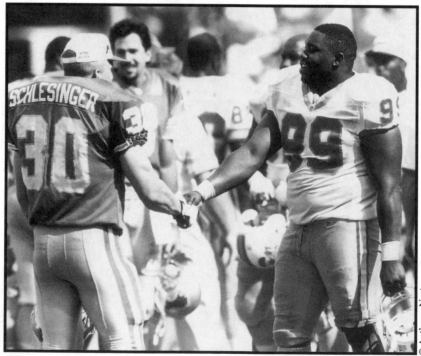

© Anthony Neste

It was a long shot. They measured it at 565. Anyway, I used to have a terrible habit . . . the funny thing about the home run is . . . that I had a terrible habit of running around the bases with my head down, you know, because I didn't want to embarrass the pitcher. I know he was embarrassed enough already, especially one that long. As I come around second, I'm getting ready to get to third base, with my head down, I hear Frank Crossetti, the third base coach, holler, "Hey, look out!" And I looked up . . . and Billy Martin was on third when I hit the ball . . . he was tagged up like it was a long fly, and I almost ran into him. Of course, he's running on into the plate laughing, and I'm right behind him.

—Mickey Mantle

If I were to choose one word to describe the Helsinki Games, that word would be "graciousness." The graciousness and kindness of the Finns toward all visitors. The graciousness of the competitors for each other; of the victors toward the vanquished; of the vanquished toward the victors.

—Brutus Hamilton, U.S. track and field coach, 1952 Olympic Games

In the 1987 movie *Wall Street*, Gordon Gekko, a Wall Street financial broker only thinly fictionalized, tells his young protégé that he's not in it for the money but because he really enjoys crushing people. Without vigilantly cultivated principles of decency and fairness, the competitive culture of Wall Street can be sadistically ruthless. But lest we blame it all on culture, consider the cruelty that young children sometimes inflict on each other. The truth is, it's a rare saint among us who has never felt the urge to crush an enemy, a rival—for that matter—a friend, a lover, a close family member.

Which is not to say we are all one step away from *Lord of the Flies* savagery—for it's just as easy to point to remarkable acts of unselfish sacrifice or charitable forgiveness instead of retaliation. But we humans are indeed capable—whether by enculturation, nature, or original sin—of ruthless dehumanization of our fellow human beings. Add to that state of affairs a competitive situation such as sport, populate it with adolescents (not to mention a few adults who are trying to relive their adolescence), and things can quickly get out of hand.

Respect for opponents is not something that young athletes will naturally develop. It will be obvious to the coach who takes the principles of sportsmanship seriously that this is a problem area. Since the central focus of every practice session and every game is to beat the opponent, it's easy to turn opponents into enemies. And, to make matters worse, since many of the opponents they face will treat them with nothing but disrespect, the natural tendency will be to respond in kind.

Many of the principles of sportsmanship we'll articulate in the following chapters are directly related to the purpose of winning, and, for that reason, they will be more obvious to the athletes. In a team sport, young athletes can easily see that they need their teammates to win. That may not automatically result in respect for them, but it certainly lays the foundation for it. Likewise, it's not hard for them to understand that a good coach is essential for winning. But, at least on the surface, the situation is different with opponents. An opponent is not someone I need, but someone I'm trying to beat—someone who's trying to foil my every effort. In order to win, I don't have to respect an opponent. Far from it. In fact, some coaches are convinced that you can't beat an opponent you have respect for.

Coach Skeptical: Look, let's be honest, kids nowadays have to pump themselves up in order to perform. That's why all of these "no taunting" rules are just silly. I'm not just talking about football or ice hockey. Even tennis players do it.

Even sprinters. When someone asked one of the American sprinters during the 1996 Summer Olympics about his screaming and chest thumping, he responded, "This is war." That attitude is certainly widespread.

Coach Skeptical: If that's what it takes for him to win, then so what?

Well, with all due respect to him, the person we're thinking of didn't win. But even if he had, isn't there a difference between trying to kill an enemy in war and trying to outrun an opponent in a footrace?

Coach Skeptical: OK, it's not really a war. But, again, if that's what it takes for him to get motivated . . .

Maybe it does, but we think it's a little more complicated than that. Bob Lilly didn't have to do war dances over his fallen opponent to convince himself to hit hard. Chris Evert didn't have to shake her fist at her opponent after winning a point to be one of the most fiercely competitive athletes in the history of tennis. If it's true that kids nowadays do have to work themselves into a violent frenzy in order to be competitive—and the truth is, plenty of kids nowadays don't— then the response is not that we have to coach or educate them differently because they are different than the kids of previous genera- tions; rather, if they are different it's because we've coached and educated them differently, and because all of the cultural forces have educated them differently. In education there's always this chicken- and-the-egg situation.

In other words, today's kids aren't different: Just like the kids of every generation, *they can learn*. They can learn to think that taunting an opponent with total disrespect is "part of the game"—or they can learn why respect for an opponent is a fundamental part of competi- tion. And, although many situations will present great difficulties for applying the principle, we can help them develop the good judgment that difficult situations require. That they can learn, of course, means that we, their parents, teachers, and coaches, can teach them. Rather than throwing up our hands and saying they're different, we can get our hands dirty and try to teach them why respect for an opponent makes sense.

WHY RESPECT OPPONENTS?

Why should I respect my opponent? On the surface, it's not obvious. It requires that we think about the nature of competition. It's only at a deeper level of understanding that we come to see that we should respect an opponent. Given that understanding we can then cultivate the *habit* of respecting an opponent, we can develop customs and rules that promote that respect; but understanding the reason for it requires that we think.

Opponents Provide Opportunities to Excel

Although it isn't at first obvious, if we do step back from the heat of battle and think about the nature of competition, the principle of respect for opponents is remarkably simple. If participation in athletic competition is valuable, then a good opponent makes it possible for me to do something valuable. No opponent, no game. In chapter 2 we argued that competition, reflectively understood, provides us with an opportunity to excel, both as athletes and as human beings. Opponents who do their best to beat me "oppose" my best effort to beat them, and on that level my opponent's best effort can be downright infuriating; however, if I step back and think about what's going on, I realize that my opponent's effort to beat me has given me an opportunity, has challenged me to do my best.

Stefan Edberg once said that one of the best matches he played was one in which he beat Boris Becker by a completely lopsided score. Since on a good day Becker was at the very least as good as Edberg, a lopsided score could only mean that Becker didn't have a good day. Since Becker was not at his best, Edberg could not have been truly challenged. In other words, Edberg could not have played his best match that day. In contrast, when Chris Evert, during an interview just after she announced her retirement from tennis, was asked what the best match she ever played was, she referred to all of the Grand Slam finals she played against Martina Navratilova. Five of those, a good tennis fan will remember, she lost to Martina at Wimbledon. Pushed to pick one match, she finally named one of the Wimbledon matches she lost as the best match she ever played. Martina brought out the best in her. It's arguable, along the same lines, that John McEnroe lost his heart for tennis when his great rival, Bjorn Borg, retired. Likewise, Muhammad Ali needed his Joe Frazier; Gwen Torrence needed her Gail Devers. Great athletes need great opponents to excel. All athletes need opponents, or they couldn't play the game; all athletes need good opponents who challenge them to excel, that is, well-matched opponents who give their best. For that reason, respect for the opponent goes to the very depths of sportsmanship.

Coach Skeptical: As I see it, an opponent is trying to take something from me. You know the saying in sports: An opponent is coming into my house. If somebody breaks into my house and tries to steal something from me, am I supposed to respect him for letting me have the opportunity to show I can protect my property? If I apply for a job and I don't get it because somebody knows the boss better, should I thank him while I stand in the welfare line?

Interesting analogies, but they don't really work. Victories in sport aren't owned like property; they're won by playing the game well. Even if you think of victory as a kind of property, it doesn't belong to anyone until the game is over. Otherwise, why play the game? For that matter, it's not even clear that a title or championship is something that you own. If you won it, last year's title will be yours forever. But when the new season begins, the title is up for grabs again, just as it was when you had your opportunity to win it.

And competing for a job isn't like competing for victory in a game. You don't compete for a job simply for the joy of competing; otherwise, every time you got a job you'd resign immediately in order to compete for another one. Sport is different, though. Although we might savor a victory or mourn a loss for a moment or two, we always want to play the game again.

Human Excellence Is Worthy of Respect

A second point needs to be made here. Far from taking away from my efforts to excel, the excellence of a fairly matched opponent contributes to my efforts; but, in addition, human excellence—whether of skill or of moral fiber—is in itself worthy of respect. If I think it's worthwhile to try to achieve excellence, then I should respect excellence in others. Even as we compete for the title, how can I not appreciate in others the achievements, the skill, or the character I so desire to see in myself? A beautiful backhand is a beautiful backhand, whether it's mine or yours; a perfect set in volleyball is a perfect set; a great effort is a great effort. Sport, then, is an arena for learning to gracefully acknowledge and to respect excellence in others. Respect for an opponent, then, also has to do with the respect for human excellence which our very decision to play the game seriously commits us to.

Coach Skeptical: I'm just afraid if you spend so much time worrying about respecting your opponent, you'll forget what you're out there for. I say forget about the opponent and think about yourself and what you're doing. You do your job as well as you can and do everything you can to win. Don't worry about the other guy!

Well, first of all competition simply doesn't work that way. It would be nice if you could just worry about what you're doing without paying attention to the opponent. But in most sports how well you do requires that you *respond* to what your opponent does—or that you make the opponent respond to what you're doing. If your opponent has an excellent backhand, you'd better take note of it. But respecting your opponent's excellent backhand doesn't mean that you'll put less effort into trying to win. It means that you aspire to hit a backhand well, too.

TIME-OUT *for Reflection*

- Come up with three stories from your experiences as a player or coach that exhibit in a striking fashion the principle of respect for an opponent—stories you might want to tell your players to give them models. Come up with three stories from your actual experience as a player or coach that exhibit in a striking fashion disrespect for an opponent.

- Are there other situations in life in which it is difficult but important to respect a person with whom you're competing? What are other situations a young person might confront in which it might be easier to see that respecting an opponent is more appropriate than, for example, hating one?

- Compare the attitude of respect with other attitudes you might take toward opponents. For example, explain the difference between respecting the opponent and liking an opponent.

- Are there ever situations in sport in which it is appropriate to fail to respect an opponent? If there are, what actions are appropriate to show this disrespect? For example, at the end of the game, should we *always*, without exception, attempt to shake the hands of our opponents? Should a coach teach players that this requirement is *absolute*?

SHOWING RESPECT FOR OPPONENTS

Once you think about the nature of competition, the general principle of respect for opponents makes sense. But what does all of this mean in practical terms?

Giving Your Best Effort

First, let's talk about what respect for opponents doesn't mean. It doesn't mean being "nice" to the opponent, although it does mean being civil. It most assuredly doesn't mean that you don't try to beat your opponent—that you don't take winning seriously. Anything less than your best effort to win is just as disrespectful as trying to win by cheating or by disrupting your opponent's mental state in ways that have nothing to do with the sport. Competition is only a "mutual striving for excellence" if both sides strive to win. I should give my best effort, and my opponents owe their best efforts to me. In fact, my respect for opponents should include demanding their best effort to beat me. If a championship (or, in the pros, a lot of money) is on the line, it's awfully tempting to be thankful if an opponent tanks it and lets me win; but we've all been in a situation, even in a weekend pickup game or a friendly neighborhood tennis match, in which we feel cheated by an opponent who gives up, drifts off, makes excuses instead of playing hard. The most conspicuous version of not giving your best effort would involve consciously deciding not to try because you're going to lose anyway. But if you have developed a temperament that causes you to give up when things aren't going well, even that in a certain sense is giving your opponent less than you should. Respect for an opponent does not mean disrespect for the spirit of competition.

TIME-OUT *for Reflection*

- Treating an opponent as an enemy to be crushed is the obvious example of disrespect for the opponent. Can you think of examples in which a superior opponent shows disrespect by only playing hard enough to win? Give examples of verbal remarks, during or after the game, through which a superior player or team might show disrespect for an inferior but honorable opponent.

- Is it ever acceptable to give less than a best effort to conserve energy?

- In an individual sport such as wrestling, is it ever appropriate to let up so as not to embarrass an opponent? In most team sports, does the custom of not running up the score go against the principle of giving your best effort? How do you resolve these two? And what about stalling in basketball when you're ahead?

Avoiding Displays of Disrespect

I owe my opponent my best effort to win, but I should do it in a way that shows my respect for the opponent's effort and my appreciation for the opportunity that the opponent's effort affords me. I should display my seriousness about competition and about winning without displaying disrespect for my opponent. Although good-natured teasing might in some circumstances heighten the competitive spirit in the best sense, as good rivalries do, there's a point at which good-natured teasing turns into disrespectful taunting and trash talking. It requires an appreciation of the particular sport, the level at which it's being played, and the background of the players to make particular decisions about where to draw this line, but it's a line that true competitors need to draw—and that good coaches need to teach them to draw. In fact, if *showing* disrespect to an opponent is the issue, then behavior that might appear disrespectful, regardless of intent, *is* disrespectful. In other words, when in doubt, keep your mouth shut. As a general rule, taunting, trash talking, and other forms of behavior that exhibit a disrespect for the opponent have no place in competition, because they display a misunderstanding of the nature of competition.

TIME-OUT *for Reflection*

- In the 1996 Olympics an American swimmer "stared down" her opponent just before a race. Would you allow your athletes to stare down opponents? Consider this question in relation to different sports.

- Do you believe it's appropriate to cheer when the other team makes a mistake?

- What can you do to encourage sportsmanship among student fans? Other fans? Parents?

- Is a player who is "cocky" disrespectful? Should you discourage cocky behavior? How?

Refraining From Gamesmanship

Because athletic competition always involves a psychological aspect, it's not easy to draw the line between acceptable tactics that disrupt your opponent's psychological balance and unacceptable gamesmanship. "Gamesmanship" is the attempt to gain a psychological edge in a manner that is not prohibited by the rules of the game, but which is nonetheless inappropriate. Gamesmanship shows disrespect for the opponent's effort to play the game well, and it also shows disrespect for the spirit of fair play.

In general, acceptable psychological strategy consists of actions that are "part of the game"—that is, using the skills that the game calls for to put the opponent at a psychological disadvantage. Gamesmanship consists of doing things that are not "part of the game" to disrupt the opponent's psychological state. Rather than using your skills at playing the game to gain the psychological advantage, you attempt to gain that advantage by remarks or behavior that do not involve the skills of the game. To draw the line between acceptable psychological strategy and gamesmanship, we have to know something about the nature and the traditions of the sport. But there is a difference. That it's easy to see the difference between obvious examples of acceptable psychological strategy and unacceptable gamesmanship shows there's a difference. That it's difficult to figure out exactly where to draw the line means that those cases that are close to the line are harder to distinguish from one another, but that doesn't mean that we shouldn't make the distinction.

If, for example, I'm playing a baseline tennis player who loves long rallies, there's nothing unsportsmanlike about serving and volleying in order to end the points quickly. That will put my opponent at a psychological disadvantage, but I'm doing it with the skills of the game. If, however, I repeatedly hold up a server who likes to serve quickly by claiming that I have something in my eye or need to adjust my strings—or, say, if I walk over to pick up the third ball, even though the server doesn't need it and it's not in my way—that probably would be gamesmanship.

TIME-OUT *for Reflection*

- Give an example from your sport of attempting to disrupt your opponent's psychological balance in an acceptable way. In an unacceptable way. Explain the difference. Or is it ever consistent with the principle of respect for opponents to disrupt the psychological balance of opponents?

Celebrating Victory Respectfully

Along similar lines, although it might be wise to accept more outward expressions of joy than the traditional Calvinist strands of Anglo-American culture have allowed, celebrations of victory that show disrespect for the opponent, without whom there would be no victory to celebrate, have no place in competition. Or, restated in positive terms, the good sport has to figure out how to express the joy of victory without showing disrespect for the opponent. One traditional answer is to take it into the locker room, that is, don't celebrate in front of the opponent at all. Even if that approach might be overly cautious, it's worth noting that it is motivated by the principle of respect for an opponent. At the other extreme, sticking your finger in the face of the defensive back whom you just beat for a touchdown pass, calling him names that don't merit mentioning here, then spiking the ball right at his feet—this sort of victory celebration (if celebration is the right word at all) exhibits an utter cluelessness about the nature of competition. Your spectacular touchdown catch was only spectacular because you beat a worthy opponent making his best effort. Suppose that he had simply stood at the line of scrimmage reciting the alphabet as you ran into the end zone uncontested and caught the pass? Would you have anything to be proud of?

TIME-OUT *for Reflection*

- After winning a game or match, in what order should players turn toward fans, friends, family, teammates, coach, opposing coach, opponents, and officials to express joy or appreciation?

- Your team has just won the state championship. Describe how you would like for your players to behave at the buzzer, with careful attention to the sequence. Describe with as much detail as possible forms of behavior that you would not like to see them engage in.

The Silver Rule

One useful test that might help to make such judgments is to apply something along the lines of the proverbial Golden Rule, which stresses the importance of attaining a broader perspective and considering the point of view of others. For centuries the development of a kind of impartiality has been seen by peoples and cultures all over the world to be central to moral education. The Golden Rule, "Do unto others as you would have them do unto you," expresses, for some, the very essence of the moral point of view. Some 500 years before Jesus offered this moral advice, Confucius probably first formulated the principle in its negative form, "Do not do to others what you do not want them to do to you." Some have called this the "Silver Rule."

For our purposes, the negative formulation is more to the point: How would it make you feel if your opponent beat you and behaved that way? If it would make you mad, then you need to rethink what you're doing. If you're playing Bjorn Borg in the finals of Wimbledon, would his falling spontaneously to his knees in a gesture of joyful reverence after winning the last point offend you? Probably not. Or let's say you're playing Martina Navratilova. Would you be offended if she clenches her fist briefly, her eyes averted downward, after making a beautiful shot, especially if she had clapped her hand against her racket strings a few points earlier to applaud a great shot you had made? Probably not. But what if your opponent runs up to the net after winning a point, or, worse, winning the match, and shakes his fist in your face?

Or consider a situation in which your victorious opponents embrace each other at the final buzzer, and maybe even dance among themselves a bit, and then come over to shake your hands with genuine appreciation for your effort. We're thinking, for example, of the Houston Rockets at the end of game four of the 1995 NBA finals. Their behavior was classy enough and respectful enough that an Orlando Magic player explained the loss after the game by saying, without the slightest resentment, that they were beaten by a better team. But what if, right after making the winning basket, your opponents run over to your bench and bump chests with expressions of hostility that call up images of cave men dancing over a mastodon they've just killed? To say it's all right because you intend to be in their position next time around misses the point.

Calculated disrespect is worse, but we also have to ask ourselves, whatever the intentions, how will a certain behavior appear? Will it appear consistent with the principle of respect for opponents? It would be nice if all we ever had to do was honestly express ourselves without concern for the effect on others or on the customs and institutions we play a part in, but the nature of competition requires that we think about how we express ourselves and that we develop the depth of character to express ourselves respectfully. The appropriate expression of joy is not an affront to others: the joy of doing something well, of participating in something exhilarating, the joy of winning. But there is such a thing as the inappropriate expression of the joy of victory. The other side of this coin, of course, is that we need to do our best not to misinterpret our opponent's legitimate celebration of victory. Simply because we wanted to win very badly doesn't mean that our opponent's joy over winning is an affront to us.

Rituals of Respect

One final point: We should never overlook the importance of ritual as a way of forming the habit of showing respect to opponents. Think of the postgame handshake, in most sports a practice that is mandatory, not according to the rules, but by custom and tradition. This ritualistic exchange is an opportunity to thank opponents for the competitive opportunity they have provided and to acknowledge their excellence.

The coach who understands the principle of respect for an opponent will demand that it be done properly. Look your opponent squarely in the eye, offer a firm handshake—not a wet noodle—and utter one of the customary remarks ("Good game," for example), and say it with conviction. The disrespectful variations of this ritual are of course endless, which means that you have to think about what you're saying. After beating an opponent badly, if you punctuate the handshake with a remark of ironic condescension—for example, saying "You played a great game" when it isn't true—you've missed the point of the ritual. If boxers routinely embrace after 10 or 12 rounds of trying to beat each other's brains out, athletes in the nonviolent and moderately violent sports can shake hands with conviction.

TIME-OUT *for Reflection*

- List the well-known rules, customs, and habits in the sports you are most familiar with that promote the habit of respect for opponents (e.g., the postgame handshake).

- Come up with sport-specific customs or rituals of your own that would promote respect for opponents.

WRAP-UP

In the end, we are again contending with the two extreme perspectives on competition that we discussed in chapter 2. At one extreme, my opponent is an enemy I try to destroy, for whom nothing but contempt is appropriate. At the other extreme, I make no effort to beat my opponent—I play "just for fun." If we understand the nature of competition, it becomes apparent that both of these views exhibit a disrespect for opponents that misconstrues the very nature of competition. Again, one is too serious and the other isn't serious enough. If I'm so determined to beat you that I can't respect your efforts to win, then I need to remember that we are playing a game; if I'm so lackadaisical about the game that I don't give you my best effort or demand your best effort in return, then I need to remember that I am participating in a competition.

CHAPTER 4

Respect for Teammates and Team

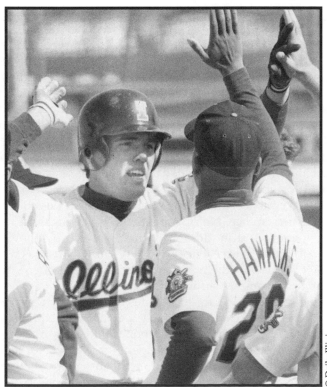

© Daily Illini

> The view that we fulfill ourselves with and through others, that we become who we can be through those involvements, is as old as the Dionysian ecstasy, as enduring as the phenomenon of nationalism, and as recent as a contemporary coach's exhortation to his players in behalf of teamwork.
>
> —Drew A. Hyland, *Philosophy of Sport*
>
> It's amazing how much can be accomplished if no one cares who gets the credit.
>
> —John Wooden

Teammates, not only opponents, compete with each other. Teammates compete with each other to make the starting lineup, to be chosen MVP of the team, to be popular with the team or the coach, to be high scorer for the game or for the season. If winning matters, teammates are necessary, and cooperation with teammates is practical; but respect for teammates is more than cooperation.

Ultimately, the most important reasons for respecting teammates are ethical, not merely practical, at least not practical in any obvious sense. I must be thankful for good teammates for the same reason I am thankful for good opponents. If participation in a team sport is a valuable experience, then my teammates make it possible for me to have that experience. No opponents, no game; likewise, no teammates, no team. And, in addition to what I get out of it, I should admire and respect human excellence anywhere I find it. Just as I respect the efforts to excel and the achievements of my opponents, I should respect my teammates' efforts and achievements.

In that sense, respect for teammates is not simply about winning. But an experienced coach knows that a great team requires—even as a pure practicality of winning—a bond among its players that involves deep respect, not merely cooperation. Respect for teammates, like respect for opponents, has to do with how we treat other human beings, win or lose; but respect for teammates also has to do with the nature of a team and of a team effort to win. Being part of a team when the team truly becomes a team, when the team "gels," is one of the great experiences of athletics. It's wonderful to witness it, and it's almost magical to be a part of it. When grudging cooperation—the honor-among-thieves version of teamwork—turns into genuine respect, the results often exceed everyone's expectations.

And, although a team gelling is in part a thing of luck and circumstance—that is, you can't force it—it doesn't happen without hard work. It doesn't happen without good thinking. And it doesn't happen without developing the *habit of respect*. Indeed, it must become a part of every practice, every team meeting, every game, every celebration, every athletic banquet.

TIME-OUT *for Reflection*

- Is it possible for a coach to overemphasize the importance of "the team"? Are there any possible dangers in stressing the values of the team as opposed to values more closely related to individual achievement?

- Is respect for teammates and team the same thing as loyalty to the team? Is there a limit to how much loyalty to the team a coach can demand?

- How do you balance respect for the team with the need for individual creativity and spontaneity?

WHY RESPECT TEAMMATES AND TEAM?

To understand respect for teammates and team, we have to understand the nature of a team effort. What is a team? A team is a group of individuals who agree to cooperate in order to achieve something *as a team*. In athletic competition, the individuals cooperate so that the team can win. To a great extent, that simply means that each individual tries his or her best. If I'm taking a three-point shot, I do my best to make it. Every basket I make is added to the score of the team. If I can steal the ball, get a rebound, or make a good pass, that contributes to the effort of the team. On this line of reasoning, if we then add up all of the individual efforts of the team members, we get the total team effort, just as you add up all of the baskets the individuals on a basketball team make during a game to get the team score. And if we turn to team competitions in individual sports, such as tennis, golf, or archery, it seems even more reasonable to say the team effort consists of the sum of the individual efforts.

Let's look first at the team version of an individual sport in which it may be harder to understand what a team effort might consist of. Consider, for example, team tennis, that is, tennis competition in which two teams compete against one another as teams (as opposed to individuals representing their schools as individuals in a district, regional, or state tournament). If one school plays another in a dual match, that means that the school that wins the most individual matches wins the dual match. If the format is six singles matches and three doubles matches, the school that wins five or more of these matches wins the dual match. Obviously, teamwork is involved in doubles. But leaving that aside for now, the "team" effort, on first examination, means nothing more than how well the singles players and doubles teams play their individual matches. The team effort is equal to the sum of the individual efforts. If our numbers two, four, and six singles players win their matches and our numbers two and three doubles teams win their matches, our team wins five of the nine individual matches and therefore wins the dual match. Simple math. . . .

Or is it? What if the two senior girls on the number one doubles team, knowing that the number three doubles match was the one that could go either way, had worked with their teammates on the number three team all week in practice, preparing them for the match? What if the number three singles player after losing her match went over to the number one player, who's sulking in the team van after losing a close match, and tells her they need to get over to the number six singles match to give their teammate some support? What if one of the lower players, who never gets to play a match but can outrun the number one player, lines up all year long next to the number one player during running drills, challenging her to keep up? If these sorts of things happen routinely, becoming a part of the team's makeup, if players do these sorts of things because they feel a commitment to the team, not merely to themselves individually, the effects do begin to "add up." Actually, they don't simply add up; they increase geometrically.

As part of a team effort in the fullest sense of the word, individuals become capable of more than they are capable of individually; and the team becomes capable of more than the sum of what the individuals on the team are capable of individually. Now apply it to a team sport, such as basketball, baseball, soccer, volleyball, or football, and this phenomenon becomes even more obvious; but the principle is the same. As the old saying has it, the whole is greater than the sum of the parts. When a team truly becomes a team, in fact, it becomes impossible to speak of summing up at all. We talk of chemistry, of gelling, of everything coming together. We talk of intangibles—we even talk about a kind of "magic."

TIME-OUT *for Reflection*

- Have you ever had a firsthand experience, as a coach or as a player, of a team coming together in a magical way? Why did it happen? What factors were involved? Try to be specific.

- Is there such a thing as the negative version of the whole being greater than the sum of the parts? Can animosity, jealousy, and other divisive attitudes among players increase geometrically?

SHOWING RESPECT FOR TEAMMATES AND TEAM

How does this magic come about? There are no guarantees, but it requires the genuine respect of the team members for each other and for the team. If I understand the nature of a team, then I recognize I have an obligation as a team member to respect my teammates and my team. What does this require? As a member of a team, I have a responsibility to play the game and to behave on and off the court in such a way as to contribute to the team's effort to win, that is, to contribute to the team's effort to play the game as well as it can. *My excellence as a team athlete, like my excellence as a human being, should make my teammates more excellent.* We'll have more to say in the last chapter about the use of sport metaphors to describe life, but suffice it to say here that if I am courageous, self-controlled, and just (to use the cardinal virtues of the classical world) and if I have good judgment in my application of these character traits, my excellence will contribute to my fellow humans. If you look at the stats of, say, Larry Bird, it's obvious he was one of the all-time greats on the basketball court; but, much more importantly, when he was on the court his teammates were better because of his presence. And as his presence made them better, he in turn drew from their higher level of spirit and play. You can't calculate it, but you can feel it: That's why we call it "magic."

Being Truthful About Abilities and Playing a Role

In order to make this kind of contribution to a team effort, players and coaches must be truthful about individual abilities and weaknesses. Everyone would love to be the high scorer, have the ball 90 percent of the time, hit cleanup, play quarterback instead of center, "kill" the ball instead of set it. But some people are better shooters than others. Some people can hit a baseball a country mile, and some can barely get it out of the infield. Some people can run like the wind and catch a football if they can touch it, and some can't run like the wind but can knock down a building if it's willing to get right in front of them. Some people were born tall and strong and can soar above the net, and some are short but have great touch.

"Playing a role" is of the essence of team sports. In some sports the roles are more clearly defined by position; in others, the roles require more judgment and honesty about abilities and limits. If I can set picks and rebound, but I can't dribble or shoot too well, I won't be the next Michael Jordan, but I might be the next Bill Russell. Or I might only be a journeyman high school basketball player making my best contribution to a team's effort to win a 1A district championship. My obligation as a team player is to figure out how my abilities fit into the team's complex set of talents and weaknesses. This includes the best use of my athletic abilities and skills *and* the contributions of my personality, spirit, intelligence, dedication—all the intangibles of character that can enable my teammates and my team to become better.

Making Individual Sacrifices and Playing a Role

In some situations, the normal roles may reverse, as Scottie Pippen apparently failed to understand in the 1994 NBA playoffs, when he refused to go back into the game because the coach decided someone else would take the final shot. The coach figured the other team would be looking for Pippen to take the shot, and he decided to use the star as a decoy—an old ploy that requires the star to understand that his role as a team member is to contribute in each situation whatever will best enable the team to win the game. Maybe Pippen wasn't being selfish; maybe he truly felt that he would hit the last shot and that his taking it was the best chance of winning the game. Should he have tried to quickly convey this feeling in the huddle without disrupting the concentration of the team? Maybe. Refusing to go back in the game didn't convey it, nor did it convey his willingness to put his own interest in stardom behind the interests of the team. Now imagine what the guy who's going to take the shot feels like, when his teammate refuses to go in the game with him? As it turned out Toni Kukoc made the shot, and the team won. A moral victory? Not really.

Respect for the team often involves some form of individual sacrifice. It's interesting that the term "sacrifice" is even used in baseball and softball as a technical term. In certain situations, an individual must sacrifice the opportunity to hit in order to advance a base runner by bunting. In virtually every sport, players are asked to assume roles, in either a specific situation, a game, or even an entire season—not just because they have no other abilities, but because the team needs them to play those roles. That requires a greater interest in team success than individual performance or statistics. When we say someone is a "team player," we are referring to a character trait: unselfishness. An unselfish player, like an unselfish person, can see the larger picture. In contrast, selfish players think about their own success when they should be thinking about the team's success. In this sense, selfish players do not respect their teams, nor the sacrifices that their teammates may be making on behalf of the team effort.

Emphasizing the Little Things

At the end of a contest, most players and fans remember who scored the most points, who ran for the touchdowns, who hit the home run, who had the most kills, or who kicked in the winning goal. But in every game there are players who do the "little things" that usually go unnoticed by fans and are rarely mentioned in the newspapers. And these little things are what make possible the "big things" that do get mentioned in the newspapers. These little things are essential for team success, and they should be pointed out and praised by coaches. Such praise reinforces the value of team contributions and the bonds that hold the team together and make success possible.

TIME-OUT for Reflection

- In the team meeting after a game, do you mention the little things that were positive?

- Think of the most glamorous part of your sport—scoring in basketball, throwing a touchdown pass in football, spiking the ball in volleyball. Then describe all of the little things that make it possible.

Coaching and Intrasquad Competition

From a coaching standpoint, respect for teammates and team means that competition among teammates—for starting roles, more playing time, top stats—must always serve the efforts of a team to be a team. Good competition among teammates can contribute to a team effort, but it must be done with that in mind. If two quarterbacks are competing for the starting position, that competition can push both of them to excel; but, beneath the competition, their efforts must be understood as a contribution to the team effort. Of course, this kind of competition can be exploited. But if it's nothing but manipulation for the sake of winning, it will often backfire in the long run, and, even if it doesn't backfire, it shows that those involved misconstrue the nature of the team. If the team wins and all of the teammates have nothing but contempt for each other because of a coach's ruthless manipulation of intrasquad rivalries, it wasn't really a team that won; it was the coach. Some victories really are hollow.

TIME-OUT *for Reflection*

- We asked you in chapter 1 if you would promote animosity between two teammates to motivate them. How would you answer that question now?

- What kinds of things can you do to make sure that competition among teammates is "healthy"?

Team Rules and Team Unity

In the end, team spirit is just that: a spirit. It cannot be manufactured or decreed. But team rules and customs can promote team spirit and team unity. The point of the rules must be clear, namely, to promote the idea that everyone on the team is a part of the team effort and that the efforts of everyone on the team must be directed toward the success of the team. For example, on virtually every team, a rule requiring players to attend all practices and show up on time is essential. Of course, the development of particular rules and customs for a particular team requires good judgment, but such judgments need to be made in light of the principle of respect for teammates and team. Arbitrary rules might create uniform team submission, but not team spirit. In each sport there are many well-known team rules that almost always make sense, but particular teams often call for remarkable creativity in devising team rules that will actually promote team spirit and unity.

And, of course, just as important as coming up with team rules is their use. Nothing destroys team unity more than an unequal application of team rules by coaches or unequal responses to them by players. Players are quick to sense when coaches have favorites or play favorites. If you're more strict, demanding, positive, or lenient with some players than others, the others will pick up on it—and resent it. And if some players take advantage of a perceived "special relationship" with the coach, the bonds that hold teammates together begin to break down. When you give special treatment to the star and when the star takes advantage of this special treatment, such unfairness ultimately is an expression of disrespect for the other players and for the team itself. A team effort requires that even though the members of the team differ in athletic ability, their responsibility to the team is equal. Greater ability does not mean less moral responsibility to the team; if anything, it means more.

TIME-OUT *for Reflection*

- Suppose you have a rule that any player who misses a practice without clearing it with you in advance will be suspended for one game. If your star player violated this rule just before the most important game of the season, would you be willing to enforce the penalty even if it meant that you would lose the game?

- Should you consult with your players before establishing team rules? That is, should you ask players to contribute suggestions concerning team rules and penalties?

WRAP-UP

Generally speaking, respect for teammates and team requires a truthful assessment of abilities. In that sense, a team effort requires that individuals sacrifice only their delusions of grandeur. But sometimes individuals may even have to hold back even though they have the ability. Respect for teammates and team requires that the individuals give their best, but it also requires the sacrifice of purely selfish interests for the sake of a greater good. In the end, though, the individuals get something back. They give strength to their teammates, but they draw strength from them. If they're lucky, they have the experience of participating in a whole that's greater than the sum of the parts. It's special; it's magical. It's hard to explain, but it's a powerful and enlightening experience. You can't guarantee it, manufacture it, force it, but you can provide an opportunity for it, and you can cultivate the character traits that contribute to it. The athlete who understands and develops this aspect of the virtue of sportsmanship will have to contend with teammates who haven't and won't, just as athletes who cultivate respect for opponents will have to deal with opponents who are disrespectful, but the principle still holds true even when the magic isn't happening. And the magic doesn't happen without the principle of respect for teammates and team. Sometimes virtue is quickly and obviously rewarded; always it is its own reward. That is, it's better to have it than not to have it. And more often than not, in a team situation respect for teammates and team, if not directly rewarded, starts to catch on. The high moral ground can be a lonely place, but sometimes it attracts good company.

CHAPTER 5

Respect for Officials

> From this fundamental law of nature, by which men are commanded to endeavour peace, is derived this second law; *that a man be willing, when others are too, as far-forth, as for peace, and defence of himself he shall think it necessary, to lay down this right to all things; and be contented with so much liberty against other men, as he would allow other men against himself.* For as long as every man holdeth this right, of doing any thing he liketh; so long are all men in the condition of war.

—Thomas Hobbes, *Leviathan*

> Boys, the rules don't make much sense, but I believe in rules. And some of us broke 'em. I broke 'em. I can't do this—I can't win like this.

—Coach Pete Bell in *Blue Chips*

Respect for officials should be one of the most obvious and least complicated components of good sportsmanship, but there seem to be fewer voices in contemporary sports calling attention to this neglected area than to issues such as trash talking, taunting opponents, or cheating. It's not uncommon for one and the same person to strongly object to verbal abuse of opponents but act as if officials are fair game for any and all manner of attacks. Likewise, it's not uncommon for the same person to consider cheating in sport a mortal sin but treat officials as nothing more than a hindrance to victory. After all, if cheating primarily involves violating the rules of the game in order to gain an unfair advantage over your opponent, and behavior toward officials doesn't directly involve your opponent, then it might seem to some people that one could be scrupulously fair in avoiding cheating while being ruthlessly disrespectful toward officials. But good sportsmanship, as we have already explained, is more than mere rule following.

Imagine this situation. You're attending a youth league sporting event—it could be soccer, football, softball, baseball, or basketball. The game is close and the competition is edgy. The parents in the stands become increasingly loud and boisterous. At some point in the game, perhaps after several questionable judgment calls by officials, the outcome is determined by yet another debatable officiating call. At the end of the game the offending official is verbally abused and literally chased out of the playing area. The irate Little League Parent—the species is not specific to baseball—is so caught up in the moment that he or she yells, screams, and is even prepared to physically confront a youth league official. This is a depressingly common spectacle in youth league sports. The game has broken down—the spell has been broken. People who generally recognize ordinary human civility have failed to live up to standards that guide their conduct in normal, everyday life. They have failed to respect officials—they have failed to respect other human beings.

As we have argued throughout this book, the key to good sportsmanship is derived from understanding the nature of what you're doing as a participant in sport. This holds for all participants, even those indirectly involved as fans. The difficulty is that participants are often so caught up in the intensity of the competition that they fail to appreciate those elements of sport that would balance their momentary passion for success and victory. Remember: Sport is both competitive and playful. It is both important and trivial. It depends not only on my own contributions; it also depends essentially on the contributions of my opponents, teammates, coaches, officials, and the traditions of the sport itself. To appreciate this requires a broader perspective. Let's distinguish between the personal perspective of the participants who see things only in terms of their own interests and a more impersonal perspective that involves seeing things in terms of other interests and perspectives. For example, in the moral education of young children, we often insist that they look at things not only from their own point of view but also from the point of view of those who are affected by their actions. We ask: "How would you feel if someone did this to you?" We ask the child to step back and view things impartially.

Precisely the same issue concerning this clash of perspectives is apparent in sport. From my personal point of view as a player, coach, or even a fan, I am usually most interested in who wins the contest. As a player I compete against an opponent to win. It is often difficult to step back, as it were, and to see my activity from a larger, impersonal perspective, one that allows me to view it more holistically or completely. Such a broader perspective would enable me to understand and appreciate the role played by and the perspective of my opponents, teammates, and coaches. Ultimately, such a perspective would include an understanding of sport itself in the most general sense, why we play our games and to what extent they matter. As we have suggested—and we can now say this a little differently—virtue in sport arises when we are led outside of ourselves, in the direction of a kind of openness to the broader picture, of selflessly seeing the way things are. And surely an impersonal understanding of sport would include an appreciation of the crucial role played by officials and *their* perspective, not simply our own single-minded devotion to succeed and passion to win.

Consider John McEnroe's behavior toward tennis officials. Of course, fans should have admired a good many of his traits as a tennis player: his fiery competitiveness, his creativity and imagination, his deft touch, his stamina. But his behavior toward officials was often inexcusable. His constant complaints about line calls sometimes turned the beauty of his matches into uncivil, shabby representations of emotional immaturity. From his point of view, he was subject to the most incompetent officiating in the history of tennis. From a broader perspective, he had an unreasonably unforgiving view of human error and an unrealistic certainty about his own perceptual judgments. As one tennis commentator put it, if he had expected the same level of perfection from himself that he did from line judges, he should have walked off the court and quit the game. His unsportsmanlike behavior was in part a function of his inability to attain a broader perspective on his play.

As it happens, we've recently had a special opportunity to experience the role of this perspective in sport. One of our good friends has worked himself up from refereeing junior high school basketball games to being the youngest referee in the Continental Basketball Association, and finally to being a referee in the NBA. It's an extraordinary experience to attend a professional basketball game after extended conversations with one of the referees. It's remarkable to see the game from his perspective as he attempts to control the game, handle the personalities, interpret the rules, reinforce the traditions, establish the "flow" of the game, and understand the psychological dynamics among the players. It is striking to interpret his judgments and appreciate the depth of his own experience and expertise from a standpoint outside the partisan perspectives of coaches, players, and fans. To put it simply, he's good. The only way to *see* this, as well as to respect the excellence he has achieved in his craft, is to attain a broader point of view. And, of course, you don't have to be the friend of an official to achieve this perspective.

WHY RESPECT OFFICIALS?

The justification of this principle is neither lengthy nor surprising. Since sportsmanship is grounded first of all in the nature of the activity, even our attitudes toward officials should reflect an understanding of sport. In organized sport officials are "part of the game." They are part of the tacit agreement that makes the game possible. One cannot have a sport contest without rules and the enforcement of rules; in an organized contest officials are the interpreters and enforcers of the conditions of competition. Officials are guardians of the spirit of the game. For that reason, respect for officials is closely related to respect for the game. Officials enforce not only the explicit rules but also the traditions and customs of the sport, the unwritten rules. Officials are often the crucial element in a system of sanctions that ensures that the rules are followed. As enforcers of equality they are there to preserve order. We should respect them for preventing the breakdown of the world of playful competition into a chaotic clash of self-serving individual wills, a "war of all against all" as the 17th-century philosopher Thomas Hobbes memorably described a competitive situation without moral constraints. In everyday life we respect police as guardians of civil order, although we wish they were unnecessary, which, of course, would only come about if we lived in a social world populated only by wholly virtuous individuals. Officials in sport are somewhat like police, somewhat like parents enforcing habits of etiquette and good manners at the dinner table, somewhat like orchestra conductors interpreting traditions and establishing aesthetic rhythms.

Officials also deserve respect for the same reasons that players and coaches deserve respect. We should respect excellence wherever it resides, and good officials embody the excellence of their craft. Just as dedicated players and coaches work hard to become better in their respective roles as sport participants, dedicated officials are seriously engaged in learning their game and attempting to be as good as they can be. Most officials share with coaches and players a deep love for their sport. Players and coaches should keep in mind that officials, by their very decision to become officials, have demonstrated a significant attachment to their particular sport. Officials aren't cynical skeptics in the sacred space of the play world; rather, they are usually fellow believers in the faith. In short, we should respect officials for their excellence, their desire to be as good as they can be, their love of the game, and their essential contributions to the event in which we're participating.

It is especially important for coaches in youth leagues, high school sports, and even in college athletics to show respect for officials and demand the same of their players. In these situations your role as a moral educator, as a *teacher* of good sportsmanship is accentuated. Here you have numerous opportunities to exhibit and reinforce habits of civility, restraint, and impartiality. It's important for you to show your players by example that they can love competition and have an intense desire to succeed and win, but that they can do this while exhibiting good sportsmanship.

Finally, respect for officials is particularly important as a defense against the loser's tendency to complain, to blame, to whine, and not to take responsibility for defeat. Coaches should *never* allow their players to make officials the scapegoats for disappointing outcomes. In the moments after a tough loss, you can help players grow as human beings by forcing them to confront their own play in the game instead of blaming officials for the outcome. And you can begin to develop in your players that broader perspective we've emphasized, by suggesting that maybe, just *maybe*, sometimes the officials are right and we are wrong.

Coach Skeptical: That's a good point about not letting players blame officials. In fact, I tell my players that they don't need to be saying anything to the officials. That's my job. But let me tell you what, it's my job to do whatever it takes to win the game. And if that means riding the official until I've got him intimidated, that's part of the game. The officials know that. It might even mean that I might say whatever it takes to get myself thrown out of the game, if we're behind and I think that's the only way to motivate my team. The officials understand that, too. It goes with the territory. If they're not willing to take a little abuse, then they shouldn't put on the stripes.

Well, what is and isn't a part of the game is largely a matter of custom and tradition. And what you're describing is probably the way a majority of coaches behave. In that sense—that is, factually speaking—

Coach Skeptical: Factually speaking?

What *in fact* do most coaches do? They probably in fact do what you're describing. But you play a part in determining the customs and traditions. What we're asking is that you think about what makes sense—what makes sense in terms of the essential role that officials play in an athletic contest. Without them, it probably won't be an athletic contest for long. What if it became an accepted practice for coaches to take out contracts on officials they didn't like? Would you say that's "part of the game"? Factually speaking, it would be. But to say it's part of the game suggests that it has something to do with what a game is, that it's part of the nature of an athletic contest. We're saying that it's part of the nature of an athletic contest that officials have an essential function, without which the game would not be a game, and that for that reason we ought to respect them.

SHOWING RESPECT FOR OFFICIALS

What we have said so far should give you more than a hint of the practical implications involved in respect for officials. But there are some obvious questions that need to be addressed, and we need more specific principles to help us make good judgments about appropriate and inappropriate complaints to officials. Does respect for officials mean that, as a coach, you could never argue, question, or complain about some officiating judgment? No, it does not. The attitude of respect does not necessitate a Pollyannish response to questionable officiating, nor does it imply Milquetoast compliance to whatever happens in the competitive arena. What, then, does it allow?

The Norms of Civil Discourse

There's no reason why relationships with officials should be governed by any other norms than the ones that govern everyday discourse. Respect for an official's judgment is analogous to respect for another's belief or opinion. I should respect your right as an autonomous human being to make up your own mind, hold your own beliefs, and govern yourself. But that doesn't mean I must agree with you or think you're always right. As a matter of fact, if I respect you as a *rational* being, that is, as a being who can reflect about matters and seek good reasons for believing things, it might mean that I feel I have an obligation to respond to your position, question it, test it, and ask for the reasons for your view. I assume that some beliefs are better than others in terms of their support, in terms of their truth; and I assume that you are interested in truth. So I might give my own reasons in an attempt to convince you you're mistaken. But this should be done with a spirit of civility, that is, with an attitude of respect. I can respect you without necessarily agreeing with or even respecting your opinion. I can engage you in a spirited and even emotional discussion without breaking the bonds of civility.

Likewise, I can respond to officials by questioning and legitimately arguing with their judgments, but I should do this without personal animosity, name-calling, or invective. I should also recognize that some judgments are more appropriately questioned than others. For example, the interpretation of rules is a legitimate area of discussion. However, constant whining about the standard "judgment calls" of an official—the strike zone in softball, offsides in soccer, traveling in basketball—is probably not appropriate. Even the response to judgment calls should be guided by the notion that officials are interested in becoming better, so your questions can help them think about and evaluate their performances. But your questions can only be helpful if officials respect *your* judgment, and continual obsessive complaints are not normally interpreted as helpful advice. In relationships in which we disagree with others, the tone of our response is crucial, and a good sport will seek to find the appropriate emotional hue of respectful reasoned disagreement.

TIME-OUT *for Reflection*

- Should you ever allow your players to question officials' calls or decisions?

- Consider this: One coach we know of insists that his players always address officials in a quite formal manner. He requires his players to refer to officials as "sir" or "ma'am," "Mr." or "Ms." Is this a good idea? Would this help to develop or reinforce a respectful attitude?

The Silver Rule

In chapter 3 we introduced the Silver Rule, Confucius's negative formulation of the Golden Rule: "Do not do to others what you do not want them to do to you." This maxim is worth considering in every situation that calls for treating others with respect, but it is particularly pertinent in this case. Players, coaches, and fans should keep this simple but profound principle in mind when relating to officials. If you would not want to be threatened, screamed at, cursed, and physically abused if *you* were officiating, then you should not behave in this manner. Broad moral rules do not always generate tidy moral judgments, but the Silver Rule should be extremely helpful in guiding practical decisions in difficult situations.

TIME-OUT *for Reflection*

- Have you considered having a prominent official in your sport come to speak to your players about the role of the official? Have you considered requiring your players to volunteer as officials for a lower level of competition in your sport?

The Principle of Charity

In logic and critical reasoning there is an important principle that guides appropriate responses to opposing positions and arguments. If you respond critically to someone, be sure you have interpreted the position accurately and reconstructed the best possible defense of it. Then if you find that there are good reasons for rejecting the position involved, you cannot be accused of attacking a "straw man," rejecting a position or argument that your opponent does not actually hold. This is a principle that encourages impartiality insofar as you attempt to accurately assess what view your opponent holds and what reasons might be given for holding it. An analogous principle might moderate our responses to officials. When responding to or assessing an officiating judgment, you should avoid the habit of continually negative responses, as if officials are *always* wrong. In fact, instant replays on television strikingly reveal how often officials are right and how often the complaints of players and coaches are misguided. A charitable openness to the possibility of the correctness of an official's judgment is an important moderating influence. Officials are neither always right nor always wrong; however, their very role involves a commitment to impartial interpretation of the rules. There's no reason to believe that they are biased in favor of your opponent, and there *is* good reason to believe that your own judgment as a player, coach, or fan may be skewed in favor of the outcomes that you desire. A charitable attitude toward officials' decisions is a practical and useful device to promote good sportsmanship.

TIME-OUT *for Reflection*

- Think of specific examples from your sport in which it is appropriate to question an official's judgment. Contrast these examples with cases in which it would be inappropriate.

- Do you agree that coaches should *never* allow their players to blame officials for a loss?

Officials and the Level of Play

A final principle should guide responses to officials in terms of how good we should expect them to be relative to the level of play at which they're participating. The principle is this: The level of officiating should be commensurate with the level of play. There's nothing vague about this principle. There is a tacit understanding among most officials that you must become *better*, as an official, if you work at increasingly higher levels of competition. We should expect high school and college officials to be better than youth league and junior high officials. Such expectations will once again act as moderating influences. At the lower levels of competitive sport, we should respond to the poor officiating of beginners and volunteers with disappointed shrugs rather than verbally offensive righteous indignation. At the higher levels, as we have said, spirited discussion is appropriate.

Of course, we can't ignore the fact that there are some bad officials. Put more strongly, some officials may be so incompetent that they should not be allowed to officiate. Whereas I must respect officials as people, I need not respect incompetence; nor must I accept the inability of an official to retain control or maintain the order of the game. Good officials deserve to be praised; bad or incompetent officials deserve a firm but civil negative evaluation, usually by their supervisors. Criticism should always take place within the proper institutional structures, but critics of particularly bad officials do neither the participants nor the sport itself any favors by passively accepting incompetence.

Finally, although our main focus here is the respect of coaches, players, and fans for officials, the implications for officials themselves should be clear. If participants and fans should only expect a level of officiating that is appropriate for the level of play, officials should make sure they are at least that good. Volunteer little league umpires may not have the time to become masters of the craft of officiating, as we would expect major league umpires to have done, but they have to know the game well enough to officiate a good little league baseball game. And, given their limitations, they have to do the very best they can, give their best effort just as we expect the players to give theirs. At any level, an official merely going through the motions is inexcusable. Every principle of respect implies a principle of responsibility: In this case, the respect we owe officials implies a responsibility on the part of officials to perform in such a way as to deserve that respect.

TIME-OUT *for Reflection*

- Have you ever officiated a sport you didn't know well—say, little league baseball—because no one else would volunteer and the kids wouldn't get to play otherwise? Were the expectations of the fans about the level of officiating commensurate with the level of play?

- As we'll explain in more detail in the next chapter, one of the most interesting but difficult aspects of sportsmanship involves the unwritten customs and traditions that develop in a sport. Are there different traditions that allow for a more or less spirited response to officials at different levels of play? For different sports?

WRAP-UP

If you've played a sport, you don't have to have a great imagination to see things from the perspective of an opponent or teammate. The perspective of an opponent or teammate is the perspective of another player. And the perspective of an opposing coach is still the perspective of a coach. We've particularly stressed the notion of gaining perspective in this chapter because the perspective of an official is fundamentally different from that of a player or coach.

We've shown that you must understand the vital *role* of the official in keeping the game a game. But we've also suggested that putting yourself in the official's shoes—either through imagination, getting to know an official personally, or through the actual experience of officiating—is an exercise that every coach, player, and fan needs to go through from time to time.

In organized sport, officials are necessary, but, as the truism of common wisdom proclaims, officials, just like players and coaches, are human. They are fallible. They are no less prone to error than coaches and players who want so badly to win, although, as we've pointed out, they are less prone to errors of bias than the players and coaches. The problem for the good sport is transparent: How do you reconcile the clash between the desire for victory and the apparent fallibility of human judgment, especially when such fallibility (real or imagined) keeps the deep desire for victory from being fulfilled? The solution for the good sport is difficult but clear: civility, sensitivity to another's perspective, charitable vision, and reasonable expectations about the craft of officiating. And we need to remember that more often than not, we find ourselves questioning the judgment of an official because the official has just reminded us of our own fallibility, of our own humanness.

CHAPTER 6

Respect for the Game

© Terry Wild Studio

To enter into a practice is to enter into a relationship not only with its contemporary practitioners but also with those who have preceded us in the practice, particularly those whose achievements extended the reach of the practice to its present point. It is thus the achievement, and *a fortiori* the authority, of a tradition which I then confront and from which I have to learn. And for this learning and the relationship to the past which it embodies, the virtues of justice, courage, and truthfulness are prerequisite in precisely the same way and for precisely the same reasons as they are in sustaining present relationships within practices.

—Alasdair MacIntyre, *After Virtue*

"You guys need to get together and remember what you're doing this for," I said. "You're *not* doing it for the money. It may seem that way, but that's just an external reward. You're doing it for the internal rewards. You're doing it for each other and the love of the game."

—Phil Jackson, *Sacred Hoops*

The 1995 *Sports Illustrated* baseball preview issue reported the results of a survey of scouts, managers, coaches, and players who were asked to name the players who are best at the fundamentals. Cal Ripken was the overwhelming winner of the "best overall fundamental player." Tom Verducci, the author of the article, spoke reverently of "players like Ripken, who respect the game and play it soundly." At the other end of the spectrum, as the 1995 NBA playoffs developed, we watched Dennis Rodman (then a member of the San Antonio Spurs) ignore his coach, mug with the fans, and even remove his shoes during a last-minute time-out with the outcome of the game still in doubt—hardly a display of respect for the game. Or, consider the fictional world of that wonderful baseball film, *Bull Durham*. Crash Davis, journeyman catcher and tutor of the talented but erratic young pitcher, Ebby Calvin "Nuke" LaLoosh, is forced to explain why he dislikes his young, undisciplined pupil. Because, Crash explains, "You don't respect yourself, which is your problem, but you don't respect the game—and that's my problem."

Compared to such basic principles as respect for opponents or respect for officials, "respect for the game" sounds less concrete, too abstract to be helpful in instructing young athletes or guiding appropriate conduct.

Yet, as the examples we've discussed show, respect for the game is an important part of the vocabulary of sports. A college track coach we know even describes the behavior of certain athletes as an "insult to the sport." And there is obviously a close connection between respect for the game and the familiar expression "love of the game." Although respect or love for a sport is difficult to explain, it may be one of the most important things you can convey to your players.

Interesting but anecdotal evidence also suggests that many of today's athletes seem to have little or no sense of the history of their sport. Some people may think that it is trivial or unimportant to know about the details of the historical development of a sport. Does it matter whether Ken Griffey Jr. knows who Curt Flood is? Who cares if an NBA player has ever heard of George Mikan? So what if an all-star guard in college or professional basketball is unaware that Bob Cousy's backcourt creativity revolutionized basketball or that Earl "the Pearl" Monroe's spin move initiated an innovative way for a dribbler to change directions? (This move is now so common that you see high school teams using it in warm-up drills before a game.)

Once again, however, we need to call attention to the significance of proper perspective. Perhaps the details, in themselves, are unimportant, but the historical perspective required to appreciate such details is not. A player may believe that a sport requires only an involvement in the immediacy of the moment; in fact, to play a sport is to become involved in a tradition. Rules are created and changed. Skills and strategies develop. Coaching becomes more sophisticated. Playing a sport necessarily involves making contact with something historically larger than the moment. Honor, prestige, and even money may come to be possessed by individual athletes, but they cannot succeed without benefiting from the past, insofar as the skills and strategies of a sport have evolved, allowing for such success. In an important sense, the goods related to becoming excellent in a given sport are shared; they are common goods made possible by the genius, effort, and triumphs of a sport's innovators and heroes. The attitude associated with an appreciation of a sport as a historical entity requires a breadth of vision that can affect the way players conduct themselves. Look, for example, at Cal Ripken or Nuke LaLoosh. Now we need to explore more fully why people in sport think respect for the game is important, and how the good sport can display such respect.

WHY RESPECT THE GAME?

If we return to Cal Ripken Jr. as an example of someone who respects his sport, we can begin to understand what this might mean and why it is important. Ripken grew up around the minor league ballparks where his father coached and managed. He heard the constant instruction in the fundamentals of the game, saw the struggles of the ball players to improve their skills, and recognized that knowledge and intensity were sometimes more important than pure athleticism. His experience generated knowledge and even a kind of wisdom about what the game demanded of its participants. He became aware of its subtleties, complexities, and traditions. "Respect for the game" is the expression we use to describe this kind of encompassing knowledge and appreciation. In a sense, respect for the game includes the full range of respect that makes up the virtue of sportsmanship. Someone who shows disrespect for an opponent, a teammate, a coach, or an official is at the same time showing disrespect for the game; conversely, a genuine respect for the game necessarily includes an understanding of the need for respecting all of its participants as essential to the game.

Underlying all of the principles of sportsmanship we have discussed is the assumption that participation in athletic competition is meaningful, valuable, worthwhile. Why else would we play? One of the reasons we owe respect, even gratitude, to opponents, teammates, coaches, and officials is that they make it possible for us to compete. They make it possible for us to participate in something valuable. The overarching concept that we use to refer to what we are participating in is "the game." And, of course, the game is more than *a* game. We may have played *a* game Friday night, but by virtue of playing that game you participated in *the* game. And just as a team effort is more than the sum of the individual efforts of the players and coach, the game is more than a particular game played on a particular day, more than a set of rules that determine how you go about trying to win, and even more than the sum of all of the individual efforts of the countless athletes who've played the game. No matter what sport we're talking about, "the game" refers to a historical entity, rich in traditions and stories, greatness and great failure, tragedy and comedy, wisdom and folly. If you pick up the bat, you're participating in the same game that Babe Ruth played. You're drawing from his greatness, and you pay tribute to it by your efforts and achievements. There wouldn't be a game without the efforts and achievements of all the participants, but the game is something greater than each of us, and probably even greater than all of us. You can't point to the game in the same way you can point to an opponent or teammates. But you can realize that there is such a thing as the game, and that it makes it possible for you to aspire to excellence, to understand something about the human condition, and to develop good character. It is the game in all its complexity that gives us the opportunity to play, and for that reason we owe our respect to the game.

Because respect for the game is less a matter of particular behavior and more a matter of an overarching attitude, the development of that attitude can have a tremendous effect on young athletes. As we have pointed out repeatedly, you must do more than teach your players the skills and strategies of their particular sport. Coaches are also educators of what philosophers once called the "passions" or the "sentiments." Coaches constantly attempt to motivate players, instill desire, generate intensity, reward effort. Coaches perpetually deal with the feelings, emotions, and basic attitudes of their players. Because the development of good character involves the development of basic attitudes, coaches who take the moral education of young athletes seriously must teach them respect for the game.

SHOWING RESPECT FOR THE GAME

Respect for the game involves an overall attitude toward the sport you're participating in, but that attitude manifests itself in a number of ways. To show respect for the game means to show respect for the rules of the game, the spirit of competition and the spirit of play, the traditions and customs that make the game what it is, and the achievements of others who play or who have played the game.

Respect for Rules

The internal goal of an athletic contest is to win the game. But what counts as winning is determined by the rules of the game. To play a sport is to engage in an activity that is defined in terms of the rules that have been created to make the activity possible. Because a game is essentially a rule-governed activity, the game itself is possible only because of an implicit agreement on the part of each participant to play by the rules. Just as the opponent makes it possible for me to excel, the rules of the game make it possible for me to play. The rules define the very activity we call a sport. Basketball wouldn't exist without the explicit rules that constitute or create the activity we call "basketball." Therefore, there is an interesting sense in which it is impossible for me to play the game, and thus to win the game, by breaking the rules, since I wouldn't be playing if I broke the rules that define the very existence of the game. (We'll say more about this curious issue later, since the norms that guide behavior in a sport are both explicit rules and unwritten customs.)

To respect a game is to respect its rules and therefore the agreement that underlies participation in the sport. To play a sport is to seek victory when the game is played, but only within the limits of the rules that have been agreed upon by the participants. For example, one of the functions of the meeting between coaches and umpires before a baseball game is to remind participants of certain rules (e.g., in high school baseball, runners must slide), make explicit agreements if some rules are in doubt (e.g., use of a designated hitter or courtesy runners), and clarify any rules specific to the particular location of the game (e.g., ground rules).

Respect for the game requires an absolute respect for fair play. It rules out cheating, that is, violation of the basic rules that define the sport: how it is to be played, what kind of equipment can be used, who can play, and so on. To cheat is to break the implicit (and sometimes explicit) agreements involved by attempting to gain an unfair advantage over your opponent. Cheating shows a lack of respect for your opponent, but it also shows a lack of respect for your sport, since the cheater seems to acknowledge that what is most important is not playing the sport as well as he or she can, as outlined by its basic rules, but winning—by ignoring those very constraints that make the sport possible. A sport sets up an arena in which an ideal equality reigns: Everyone is equal in relation to the opportunities or possibilities provided by the rules. Cheating disrupts this equality and thus disrupts the underlying conditions of the sport. Hence it is important for a coach to insist that respecting or loving your sport means that a player be committed to the goal of winning, not by any means necessary, but only by those means permitted by the often unimaginably complex possibilities allowed by the rules of the sport.

TIME-OUT *for Reflection*

- It is often difficult but appropriate to distinguish between breaking rules for strategic reasons (e.g., in basketball intentionally fouling a poor free throw shooter in the final moments of a close game) and cheating, that is, breaking rules in order to gain an unfair advantage over your opponent (e.g., knowingly playing an ineligible player). Examine this distinction by considering a number of examples from your sport. Is this an important distinction?

- During a head-to-head archery match in a single-elimination bracket, one archer's spotting scope falls over in the high wind and breaks. Since they're shooting at a target 70 meters away, without a scope or binoculars it's impossible to see where the arrows hit the target. Seeing what has happened, the other archer is generous enough to call the location of the opponent's arrows. According to the rules, however, an archer may not give or receive assistance while on the shooting line. Is the archer who gives this assistance or the one who receives it acting in an unsportsmanlike fashion?

Respect for the Spirit of Competition

Sport is not mere frolic—it involves a contest. In sport there are winners and losers. Some may think these points are so obvious that they need not be mentioned, but, as we've discussed, there are critics of sport who think that competition is inherently bad. They want the conditions of sport changed at various levels in order to lessen the so-called damaging effects of competitive activities. But many of the positive aspects derived from sport are generated by the inherent struggles and tensions associated with engaging in a contest. Because something is at issue when one plays in sport—namely, winning the game or contest—a respect for the competitive atmosphere of sport demands that players attempt to play as well as they can, with intensity and devotion. A respect for competition means that a player must not give up even under the most undesirable circumstances (e.g., being soundly thrashed by a better player or team), and a superior player or team should never allow the contest to degenerate into disrespectful festivity simply because the score is lopsided.

Respect for the competitive nature of sport is especially important when teams are mismatched and a team or player is winning or losing badly. Players who respect the game or respect their sport must continue to play as well as they can although the conditions of the contest may be imbalanced. Respect for competition might also come into play when a coach is deciding a lineup before a game. For example, a coach who thinks there is no chance of beating a particular team might play the weakest players on the squad as a way of showing that the game doesn't really matter. In this case, the coach fails to respect the sport by denying its basic competitive thrust. To seek victory in sport by playing as well as you can at all times may not be the *only* reason to participate in a sport, but it is surely an essential part for anyone who loves or respects a sport. As we have repeatedly insisted, all of the other reasons you might have for participating require this dedication to the spirit of competition.

Vince Lombardi is often quoted as saying, "Winning isn't everything—it's the only thing." Bart Starr claims that Lombardi actually said, "Winning isn't everything—but making the effort to win is" (Walton, p. 4). Even that remark is a bit of locker-room hyperbole, for, indeed, there are other things that matter in sport besides making an effort to win. But by the very nature of competition, the competitors are obligated to make that effort. Making an effort to win is not everything, but it is an essential part of respect for the game.

TIME-OUT *for Reflection*

- We have argued that giving your best effort is part of what it means to respect the spirit of competition. What else goes into respect for the spirit of competition? Can you give examples from your experience that demonstrate either respect or disrespect for the spirit of competition?

Respect for the Spirit of Play

Although participation in sport sometimes involves hard work, sacrifice, and single-minded commitment, you should never forget that sport is a form of human play. As we have suggested, sport resides in the neighborhood of play. Unlike activities whose value rests primarily in the way they bring about other valuable or useful things, playful activities are intrinsically valuable. In other words, they are valuable in themselves. As philosophers have said, play is *autotelic*—that is, it is an activity whose goal or purpose is internal to itself rather than external or instrumental. We choose to play because of the joy, pleasure, satisfaction, or fun of the activity itself. In contrast, we work because we must, in order to survive or to live well, so we often fill our lives with hours of toil. Most of us would like to be able to devote ourselves to activities that we would choose to engage in if we were freed from the necessity of working (or, perhaps the best of all possible worlds, to find work that we view as intrinsically valuable). On the one hand, as an activity we freely choose to engage in, play is an arena of liberation and, at its best, joy and affirmation. On the other hand, since play is not an instrumental activity, it produces nothing. It is in this sense quite literally useless. Although it may be put in the service of other human values, for example, when it is used as entertainment in professional sports or when it is used to promote nationalism in the Olympic Games, from the standpoint of various worldly matters like economics, politics, and religion, play is trivial.

Coaches usually do not need to be reminded that sport is competitive, but it is crucial to remind some that it is competitive *play*. Sport is by its very nature paradoxical. It demands that we compete as hard and as fairly as we can, yet that we do this while realizing that sport is play, a set of captivating and intrinsically valuable activities that do not matter in the larger scheme of things. I must play my sport as if nothing matters more than swimming or pitching or putting better so I can win, all the while realizing that it doesn't really matter, from another standpoint, that I succeed. Thus players and coaches must seek to find the proper balance between competitive seriousness and the spirit of play. From the perspective of sportsmanship, understanding the paradoxical nature of sport produces both a sense of fair play and an attitude of generosity and playfulness. If competitiveness is sometimes needed to temper a lack of seriousness or effort on the part of some players, the spirit of play is needed to moderate and guide a sense of competitiveness that may sometimes be too harsh and unrelenting, as if winning by any means necessary is the only purpose of sport participation.

Coach Skeptical: I still have trouble saying that sport is play. That makes it sound so childish. Sport is about competition—it's about winning and losing. It's not about tinker toys and dolls.

Undoubtedly, there are different kinds of play, from the spontaneous running and jumping of children to the more formal rule-governed, competitive play of sport. To say that sport is a form of play is not to reduce it to the frolic of children. To stress the playful character of sport is to appreciate the valuable and even joyful possibilities of participating in such activities, regardless of their value in producing other goods, like money, prestige, honor, fame, or even the momentary satisfaction of victory. From the standpoint of play, what's important in sport is the process not the product, the activity, not merely the consequences.

Respect for the playful character of sport should produce an attitude that rules out such behavior as taunting, trash talking, and fighting. Think of situations in which small children's play may degenerate and you must remind them that "It's only a game" and that there's something silly about acting as if it mattered so much. Likewise, when players get older, it's often important to remind participants that they're playing *games*, not fighting enemies. One very successful college baseball coach has argued that the traditional postgame handshake between teams should be postponed (or even eliminated?) because the participants need a "cooling-off period" after intense competition. Respect for the playful character of sport should produce all the cooling off a player or coach might need in order to relate to his opponent generously and gracefully after a victory or a difficult defeat. To repeat, if boxers can embrace each other with genuine enthusiasm at the end of a fight, which they often do spontaneously after a good bout, baseball players can shake hands without a cooling-off period.

TIME-OUT *for Reflection*

- What are the most significant threats to the spirit of play in sport? Can you distinguish between the threats that come from the very nature of competition and those that come from external sources?

- As a coach what can you do to instill the spirit of play in your players? Parents? Fans? Administrators?

- As a coach do you ever set aside some part of your practice for activities that are pure "fun"?

Respect for the Game's Traditions and Customs

One of the most interesting and important aspects of respect for your sport arises because a sport is more than simply a collection of explicit rules laid down at a certain time. A sport is not a static, tightly defined set of behaviors. A sport is a historical entity. It grows and develops. As skills are improved and more is learned, players and coaches develop innovative strategies to respond to opponents. Both teaching and learning your game become more complicated and increasingly sophisticated. Recognizing the deeply historical nature of a sport or game is crucial for sportsmanship, because respect for rules must be understood in the context of both the explicit written rules and the unwritten customs that arise in the development of a sport.

Being a good sport does not require strict, saintly obedience to every written rule. For example, consider this common situation in basketball. In the fourth quarter of a close basketball game, a player steals the ball and goes in for a layup. What should a defensive player do? If she understands the situation and has been well-coached, she fouls the offensive player as hard as is necessary in order to keep her from shooting an uncontested layup. The defensive player forces her opponent to make two free throws instead of allowing her to score easy points. There's nothing mysterious about this example. Such a foul is not bad sportsmanship, and it calls for no angry response by the players, coaches, or fans of the opponent's team. Here an explicit rule is violated, but the customs of the sport arising from strategic necessity demand that a player violate the rule. Note, however, that here the rules also allow for the appropriate penalty.

Knowing what is and is not appropriate in the context of the customs of your sport is not always an easy matter. It requires knowledge, experience, and good judgment. To make things even more difficult, customs change. In baseball at one time it was thought to be "bush league" for a team to attempt to steal bases when it was ahead by four or five runs or more. Now it's more acceptable to attempt to steal bases when a team is considerably ahead, although there is a point, as a matter of good judgment and respect for the game, at which this becomes inappropriate. In baseball it's permissible to steal signals, break up a double play hard at second base, throw inside, and quick-pitch; however, it's contrary to the customs of the sport to squeeze when you're far ahead, attempt to injure an infielder by sliding with your spikes high, or yell "swing" as the ball crosses the plate during a game. For players and coaches, these matters are directly related to sportsman-ship. To say that these actions are contrary to the customs of baseball is to say that it would be *unsportsmanlike* to do them. Only ignorance would excuse a person from being judged this way.

Every sport has its subtleties and nuances. It's important for you to convey to your players that the game has a historical life of its own, which they must understand and respect in order to be good sports, not just good players. And, of course, participation in anything that has a histori-cal life means that we must learn and conform ourselves to established traditions, while at the same time recognizing—and taking responsibility for—the way in which our decisions, judgments, and actions contribute to an ongoing tradition. How I behave on the playing field today and how I interpret the rules and customs and traditions of the game today will play a role in the creation of the customs and traditions for future players.

Generally speaking, then, respect for the game requires a respect for and adherence to the established customs of the game; but that doesn't excuse us from the responsibility for the formation of new customs. In fact, in some situations the expression "It's part of the game" can become an excuse for behavior that is totally contrary to the very concept of a game. Sometimes administrators, coaches, and players need to step back and make the judgment that something has become a part of the game that shouldn't be. There's no reason, for example, that regular fist fights should be a part of hockey; no reason shouting insults at chair umpires should be a part of tennis; no reason bench-clearing brawls after every inside pitch should be a part of baseball. Precisely because customs and traditions are so much a part of particular sports, especially for young people learning their games, all the participants need to take seriously their roles in the formation of those customs and traditions for the next generation. That may seem like a confusing catch-22 of a predicament; but if it is, it's a predicament humans face in virtually everything they do.

The upshot of what we have said about respect for traditions and customs of a game is this: Whenever you hear the phrase, "It's part of the game," or whenever you use it yourself, you must be very careful to relate it to other central aspects of sport and sportsmanship as well as to broader moral norms. For example, showboating and trash talking have, as a matter of fact, become a part of the game in many sports. But that doesn't justify the behavior. These actions conflict with respect for opponents, the very nature of athletic competition, and, perhaps more importantly, the most common, everyday norms of human decency and respect for others. There's no reason to leave behind the central concerns of moral character when we play sports. The truth is just the opposite.

TIME-OUT *for Reflection*

- How do certain forms of behavior become "part of the game"? Who's to say? How is a tradition established? Can you think of examples?

- Come up with examples from sports you know well of unacceptable forms of behavior that have become common practice. Then explain why these forms of behavior should not be part of the game and why young players ought to be taught not to behave in these ways. Then come up with traditions and customs in the same sports that properly guide players' actions and are therefore appropriate parts of the game.

Respect for Achievement and Excellence

One final aspect of respect for your game or sport arises both from its historical nature and from the fact that it is a competitive activity with standards of excellence. When kids begin to play a sport, it's not long before they realize that some players are better than others. Coaches, of course, attempt to teach their players how to become better. It is also important and often humbling for players to learn to recognize real quality in the way their sport is played and to make accurate, that is, realistic judgments about their own abilities and the abilities of others. Such judgments are important not simply because they produce humility and realistic expectations, they are also significant because they generate the desire to develop skills in response to weaknesses in various abilities. But they are also crucial in response to competition with opponents, because accurate judgments about who plays well and who doesn't, about who is *good*, generate an appreciation of excellence.

As any player knows, losing is difficult. It is often difficult to face our own weaknesses, so we make excuses. We rationalize and we blame. Our opponent was lucky. The officiating was poor. We had an off-day. The excuses proliferate. However, a proper respect for achievement requires that I give credit where it is due. When I am beaten by a superior opponent, I should not make excuses and I should not whine. Respect for excellence means that I must accept responsibility for defeat when it is in fact caused by an opponent who played better or *was* better—at least at that time. To respect my game or sport requires admiration (even grudging admiration!) for the present achievements of participants.

Finally, insofar as a sport also has a history of past achievements, respect for the game involves respect for those who have played it best. This is the right place for heroes, in sport as elsewhere. Heroes are noteworthy not because of their income, celebrity status, or awards. Instead we should admire them as exemplars of excellence. Appreciation of heroes is appreciation of excellence. They show us what is possible in some area of human endeavor. Recall that we mentioned earlier that coaches are more than simply physical educators: They are also educators of attitudes and desires. Respect for past achievements as embodied in heroes involves opening yourself to the breadth of possibilities in your sport. George Will has an insightful comment in regard to this concept:

> It requires a certain largeness of spirit to give generous appreciation to large achievements. A society with a crabbed spirit and a cynical urge to discount and devalue will find that one day, when it needs to draw upon the reservoirs of excellence, the reservoirs have run dry. A society in which the capacity for warm appreciation of excellence atrophies will find that its capacity for excellence diminishes. (p. 329)

Respect for the game involves the "largeness of spirit" that Will speaks of. We need our heroes in an age of cynicism, and we need to teach our children to admire the good, not merely the rich and famous. Coaches can play a useful role here by stressing respect, admiration, warm appreciation, and other positive attitudes in response to the present and past achievements of players.

TIME-OUT *for Reflection*

- When we speak of the great heroes of a sport—say, Babe Ruth in baseball—is that the same thing as talking about role models? What is it we admire—or that we should admire—about the all-time great players of a game?

- After a game do you discuss the things your opponents did well when you're talking to your players?

WRAP-UP

The players who embody a genuine respect for the game exhibit the "largeness of spirit" that George Will talks about. Respect for rules, the spirit of competition and the spirit of play, the traditions and customs of the game, the achievements of others—seeing ourselves as participants in something greater than each of us individually could achieve, even greater than the sum of our individual achievements, enlarges us. Restricting the ego sometimes means enlarging the spirit.

CHAPTER 7

Respect Between Players and Coach

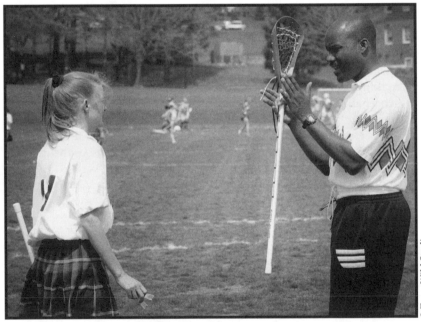

© Terry Wild Studio

> . . . Rational beings are called persons inasmuch as their nature already marks them out as ends in themselves, i.e., as something which is not to be used merely as means, and hence, there is imposed thereby a limit on all arbitrary use of such beings, which are thus objects of respect.

—Immanuel Kant, *Grounding for the Metaphysics of Morals* *(Ellington translation)*

> I had hated him at times during training camp and I had hated him at times during the season, but I knew how much he had done for us, and I knew how much he cared about us.

—Jerry Kramer on Vince Lombardi

Imagine this situation. At the beginning of the game a junior college basketball coach tells the point guard not to take a shot without first making a pass. The point guard is the star of the team and the high scorer almost every game, but the coach explains that he needs to get the rest of the team involved in the offense. If you run the offense, the coach explains, the ball will come back to you plenty of times, and for open shots. The first time down, the point guard crosses the line and jacks one up from two steps behind the circle. As he runs by the bench getting back on defense, the coach jumps up and yells at him to run the offense, make the first pass. The player yells an obscenity back at the coach loud enough for half the gym to hear.

Well, we asked you to imagine this situation—but, in fact, it's not an imaginary situation. It happened pretty much as we just described it. And this sort of thing happens all too often. The end of the story is even worse than the beginning. The coach, knowing that the team had no chance to win without the star player, put up with this disrespect. He left the player in the game, and the player continued to disregard the coach's instructions. The player failed to exhibit respect for his coach, and the coach failed to demand respect from the player.

Now imagine this scenario. The high school softball team plays for the district title against their arch rival. After three losing seasons in a row, the coach wants this title desperately. There's even talk around town that if she doesn't win district this year, she might be looking for a job. But the arch rival has one of the best pitchers in the state. The girls get the bat on the ball, but only get three hits, one of them a perfect leadoff bunt. They advance one of the runners to third, but never score. One girl gets thrown out at second on a steal that the coach called. They play flawless defense. Their pitcher throws a brilliant five-hitter, and the arch rival scores one run. They lose a hard-fought, well-played game. Back in the locker room after the game, the coach goes ballistic. She tells her players that they didn't want it bad enough, calls them a bunch of babies. She yells at the player she sent down to second, telling her she's so slow she looks like a pregnant turtle running. "You're pathetic!" she yells, then storms out of the locker room.

This coach failed to show respect for her players. But in order to deserve the respect that you should demand from your players, you have to treat them with respect. Disrespect for players, as we'll see, can take many forms. The abusive coach who is more concerned about his or her own record is the obvious case, but the coach who simply doesn't care is equally disrespectful. One of our students recently told us that his high school golf coach would play a round with his buddies while the players were competing in match play, totally ignoring them.

In this chapter, we'll discuss the role of the coach in a team effort first, then the respect of players for the coach, and, finally, the respect of the coach for the players.

THE ROLE OF THE COACH

Just as players, by the very nature of competition, must respect the authority of officials, they must respect the authority of their coach. Authority is the legitimate use of power over others. The abuse of that power sometimes tempts us to believe that all authority is a bad thing, and that we should seek coach-player, teacher-student, and parent-child relationships that are free of authority. The truth is, if you're a coach, you have authority over the players. It can be shaped and developed in different ways, but it can't be avoided. For a coach, just as for a teacher or parent, to renounce authority is to abdicate responsibility. We'll first discuss the authority of the coach and the respect players must have for that authority, but only as a prelude to a discussion of the coach's responsibilities to the players, which, as we've mentioned, we'll discuss in the final section of this chapter.

Part of the authority of a coach comes from the nature of sport. In a team sport especially, many of the decisions, by the very nature of the game, must be made *on behalf of the team* by a coach. If you've ever played in a basketball league on a team without a coach, you know the advantage of having a coach decide who goes in the game and when, what defense to play, or who should take the last shot in a close game. Ten or fifteen people can't make split-second decisions of that nature—they all want to be in the game or they wouldn't be there, and they all were hall-of-fame coaches in a previous life. In that sense, a coach is an integral *part* of a team effort. The authority of the coach to make decisions on behalf of the whole team is greater than that of any of the players, but the coach's authority derives from the nature of a team effort.

But the authority of a scholastic coach, and therefore the responsibility, is far greater. Whatever the entertainment and financial value of school athletics, there can be only one justification for schools fielding athletic teams—the educational value of participating on those teams for the students. Scholastic coaches are first and foremost educators, teachers of young people. They must understand the place of sport within an academic setting—but that means more than merely keeping sport from interfering with academics. It means that sport ought to *contribute* to the educational goals of the school. If coaches are often granted greater authority over young people's lives and greater autonomy in their work than other teachers (a discrepancy that probably bears some serious rethinking), that should mean, not that winning football games is more important than learning geometry, but that coaches have a greater responsibility to broadly influence the lives of students. Simply put: more authority, more responsibility. As we discussed in part I, teachers of all kinds are moral educators, whether they acknowledge it or not, but there's certainly no getting around it for coaches.

THE PLAYERS' RESPECT FOR THE COACH

Because of the role of the coach, as an integral part of a team effort and as an educator, one of the principles of sportsmanship must be respect for the coach. For some group efforts, freewheeling discussion makes sense; for some, a commanding officer, a leader, a coach is essential. Team efforts in athletics require both discussion and the leadership and authority of a coach, and a sense for which is appropriate when. Just as a team cannot truly be a team without the respect of teammates for each other, without the players' respect for the coach there cannot be a team. They don't necessarily have to "like" the coach, but they do have to respect the coach—which means that they have to treat their coach with respect. Although as a player I may not be blessed with a John Wooden or a Bud Wilkinson, the underlying principle of my relationship to my coach is respect. I may disagree with particular decisions, and I may even express that disagreement; but, if I agree to play the game, to be on the team, I have to understand and respect the role of the coach in my team's effort to win.

If a coach goes beyond the bounds of propriety, I may quit the team or even work for that coach's removal; but, otherwise, this is the coach I'm stuck with, and my respect for him or her is essential for a team effort to work. Many a parent, and maybe a few athletic directors, have correctly pointed out to a disgruntled young athlete that learning to work with a bad coach is not unlike a good many situations in life. Of course, many a parent has worked to undermine the authority of a coach, and, needless to say, in youth athletics the support of parents is essential. Support here primarily means staying out of the way and letting the child have the experience of playing on a team and playing for a coach, even a difficult one. It ought to be sobering for the players to recognize that the coach is stuck with all of them as well. And it may sometimes be sobering to find out that the coach turned out to know what was what, even if it wasn't obvious at the time. One of the rewarding experiences for a coach occurs when the former players become coaches themselves and come back to confess their newfound respect for the coach who once, supposedly, made their lives miserable. Just as it is helpful for players to try to see the game through the officials' eyes, they need the perspective of seeing it through their coach's eyes as well.

Respect for a scholastic coach is also respect for a teacher. Again, I may not think the world of the particular moral educator I've been blessed or cursed with. We can all cite counterexamples of coaches who build bad character, but the truth is, most coaches, like most teachers, are individuals who've dedicated their lives to the education of young people, sometimes with great reward, sometimes not. Coaches, like teachers, are fallible human beings, but by virtue of the role they've been willing to accept, they deserve the benefit of the doubt with regard to respect.

Of course, the principle of respect for coaches as teachers throws us back into our chicken-and-the-egg educational situation again. If that respect has declined, it's because we haven't taught respect. The upshot of this discussion is that it is the responsibility of coaches to teach respect for legitimate authority in part by demanding respect for themselves as coaches and as educators. Anything less teaches disrespect. To say that kids now don't respond to authority as previous generations did is probably true; but that means it must be taught— creatively, perceptively—but taught. A part of teaching respect is to teach what counts as *treating* someone with respect. As we'll discuss in the next section, respect is based in part on understanding and perception, on an evaluation of merit, but it's also partly a matter of habit and practice, a matter of ingrained character. In some cases, treating a person with respect is no longer the reasonable thing to do—

in the late 30s and early 40s, for example, Adolf Hitler deserved nothing but contempt—but, generally speaking, treating people with respect is a good habit to cultivate.

In this arena, the two extreme approaches to sport we discussed in chapter 2 manifest themselves as *undercoaching* and *overcoaching*. We'll have something to say about overcoaching in the next section. Undercoaching means abdicating the responsibility of authority, restructuring the coach-player relationship so that the coach has less responsibility, especially as an educator. There are many versions of responsible coaching, just as there are many personalities—some of them Bobby Knight ferocious and some of them John Wooden saintly—but a coach who accepts the responsibility that comes with the coaching territory must structure the coach-player relationship as a relationship of authority. It may become a friendship, but it's closer to parenthood.

Thus far we've emphasized the need for a coach to *demand* respect. Of course, a big piece of this puzzle is still missing. A coach who doesn't demand respect of the players is shying away from the responsibilities of coaching; but a coach who merely demands it will fail to get it. With the demand for respect comes the responsibility to be worthy of it. When you answer to the first kid who extends the respect of calling you "coach," you've made a commitment to return that respect. We've dwelled so long on the authority of coaches because the only reason to grant authority to coaches is in order for them to contribute to the education of our children. Underlying the principle of respect for coaches, however, is the respect that all educators should have for the potential of their students to learn.

TIME-OUT *for Reflection*

- Can you think of examples you have experienced or witnessed of players showing disrespect for a coach?

- Do you allow players to call you by your first name? What form of address do you require of them?

- List some forms of showing respect to the coach that you think are appropriate for a coach to demand of players up front. List some forms of showing respect for the coach that could only be expected as a result of the coach's having earned respect.

- How do you draw the line between demanding proper respect and excessive authoritarianism? Can you think of examples of each?

THE COACH'S RESPECT FOR THE PLAYERS

What, then, do you owe the players in order to be worthy of their respect? You owe it to them to know and teach the game and to understand, teach, and exhibit the virtue of sportsmanship. Anything less is undercoaching. By the same token, you owe it to them to resist the temptation to overcoach. In other words, you owe it to them to exhibit and to teach the proper balance of seriousness and playfulness that athletic competition calls for.

Knowing and Teaching the Game

If coaches, as an integral part of a team effort, must make decisions on behalf of the team, then they have to know the game. And that means no matter how well you know the sport, you owe it to the players to be a lifelong student of the game—of its new developments as well as its old nuances. We know of no sport that any one individual has understood perfectly. And, in some cases, you may have been hired as an assistant football coach, but the school decides to field varsity golf teams and you get the assignment. You know the word "birdie" is used in a peculiar way in the golf world, but beyond that, not much. You can't fake it with kids who know the game, but, within the constraints of your other responsibilities, you can make a commitment to learn the game. There's a big difference between walking out on the green and saying, "I'm new at this game, but I'm going to learn it as fast as I can," and saying, "This isn't my main job, so you'll pretty much be on your own." Coaches have a responsibility to know, and therefore to learn, their game. The split-second decision of a coach who is clueless about the game is hardly an improvement on all the players talking at once. Better no coach than a clueless one.

Coaches must be students of the game in order to make coaching decisions based on sound knowledge, and, especially in school athletics, they must be students of the game because they have a responsibility to teach the game to the players. Respect for the players as students of the game, as young people with the potential to learn, means that scholastic coaches are never just recruiters. And, indeed, one of the most exciting aspects of coaching young people is to see them develop as players. Every coach should look in the mirror at the end of each year and ask these questions: Are my players better at the game than they were at the beginning of the year? Are their skills better? Do they understand it better? Have they learned the game?

That's not an easy task, because teaching the game is not an easy task. Some players want to learn, love to learn; some are convinced that they know everything there is to know. Some positively resist instruction, refuse to take seriously the practice drills that develop skills, prefer to look cool rather than poised. Respect for the players' potential to learn, then, doesn't mean giving them whatever they happen to want, because some of them will want to play the game without learning it. The one advantage a coach has over other teachers, though, is that there is a clearly defined goal that all of the players want, namely, to win.

TIME-OUT *for Reflection*

- What does it mean to be a "student of the game"? Are you a student of the game? What do you do to keep learning your game?

- Do coaches have an obligation to attend coaching clinics and meetings in order to gain knowledge about their sport? To read the latest literature on their sport?

- Are your players more knowledgeable about the game after playing for you for a season? After playing for you for several years?

Understanding, Teaching, and Exhibiting the Virtue of Sportsmanship

Coaches exhibit respect for their players and they merit the respect of their players by knowing and teaching the game. But the responsibility runs deeper than that. If you think about the nature of competition, and about its role within an educational setting, if you *understand* what it means to compete, you will recognize that respect for your players means, above all, taking responsibility for teaching them the principles of sportsmanship. How? Depending on the age and the character of the players, the balance will differ; but teaching sportsmanship will always involve some combination of explicit instruction, example, and opportunities for practice.

Coach Skeptical: If my job depends on winning the district title, I don't have time to set aside for sportsmanship lessons. Every minute I'm allowed to spend with my players—and there's not enough time as it is—I need to be concentrating on playing the game well.

First of all, if you think about what it means to play the game, then sportsmanship is part of playing it well. But we also want to be clear here: We're not talking about setting aside separate practice sessions on sportsmanship. In talking about explicit instruction, setting an example, and practicing sportsmanship, what we're really asking you to do is to coach in light of the principles of sportsmanship—to run your drills and practices and coach the games in light of these principles. It won't take extra time, and it won't distract from your efforts to win—it might mean that you'll do the things you've always done differently, though.

Teaching by Explicit Instruction. Talk about sportsmanship. Explain it. Don't assume that kids can't understand. Why should you treat an opponent with respect? Because no opponent, no game. Do you want to play the game or not? Do you get something out of playing the game or not? Direct moral exhortation alone is not enough, but in this age of compulsive psychological engineering, it's often short-changed. Tell them something's wrong or right, tell them why it's wrong or right, and say it like you mean it. Sometimes it's a real eye-opener for them.

When asked what he told his athletes, Brutus Hamilton, the head coach of the U.S. track and field team for the 1952 Olympic Games, said:

> The gist of my talks with the boys can be reduced to a few simple words, "Honor yourselves, your country, and your opponents with your very best performances and with your very best behavior." (Walton, p. 105)

Depending on the coach and the situation, saying it like you mean it might involve a reserved seriousness—or it might involve some heartfelt shouting. If you do express anger at players, a good self-check is to ask yourself if you're yelling at them because they lost a game or kicked a ground ball—or because they did something unsportsmanlike. Did they make a mistake or did they do something *wrong*? If they lost the game or dropped the fly because they made a halfhearted effort, that's an issue of sportsmanship; but if they played the game or went for the ball with all of the skill they possess (that is, that you've taught them), and they still lost or flubbed it, then what's the point of treating them as if they did something morally wrong? Ask yourself if you're really mad at them because they did something wrong—or if you're mad because *you* didn't get to chalk up another one in the win column? Are you yelling at them to show everybody in the stands that it's their fault, not yours—or to teach them?

Teaching by Example. Preaching without practicing what you preach is better than neither, especially if you're occasionally honest enough to admit that you didn't live up to what you preach. But the example that coaches set in the arena of sportsmanship cannot be overestimated. If you insist that the players "behave"—that is, at least on the surface, appear to respect opponents, teammates, officials, and their coach—but they see you treat others with nothing but disrespect, the lesson is all too clear. What they learn is that when they get to be the one in charge, they can treat others any way they want to. It's only when someone with power over them forces them to behave this way that they should do it, not because it's better or because they'll be better human beings for doing it.

What will players make of your demand that they treat the officials with respect when you repeatedly do the opposite? The coach in most sports may, by custom at least, have a special license to complain to the officials, but a coach can complain in ways that are consistent with respect for the norms of civil discourse—as opposed to complaining in ways that show no understanding of the nature of competition. What will players make of your demand for respect when, even at the deepest level, you treat them with disrespect? There's no denying that coaches have a special authority over players that players don't have over them, which means that coaches must sometimes make decisions that are unpopular with the players. But the question still remains: Do you exercise your authority in ways consistent with respect for your players, as students of the game and of life, as fellow human beings, as kids with the potential to learn?

On this score, we recommend the proverbial conversation with the mirror after every practice and every game. The appropriate question: What did my behavior teach them about sportsmanship?

Practicing Sportsmanship. If sportsmanship is a virtue, it can be practiced. Coaches have a responsibility to make the workouts as well as the games occasions for the practice of sportsmanship. Every good coach knows that even though an occasional light workout is a good idea, generally speaking, halfhearted efforts in daily practices will become a habit of halfheartedness that translates into halfhearted efforts in competition. Likewise, even though occasionally allowing players to let off steam in practice is probably a good idea, if you allow your players to show disrespect for opponents, teammates, or the game in daily practice you'll find that they have developed the habit of disrespect. If it's OK for them to throw their rackets when they're playing a teammate in a practice match, then how could it not be OK to do it during a match? Even if it's not OK, it's a tough habit to break. Not many people know that when Bjorn Borg started playing tennis as a teenager in Sweden, he had a bad temper. After one outburst on the court, his coach sent him home for a couple of weeks and told him that when he came back one more episode would result in a permanent expulsion from the tennis club. As most people know, no tennis player in the history of the game conducted himself with greater dignity than Bjorn Borg did during his career.

TIME-OUT *for Reflection*

- Is the teaching of sportsmanship a part of your coaching? What are the specific ways in which you reinforce the value of sportsmanship?

- Do you discuss issues of sportsmanship with your players? At the beginning of the season? When the occasion calls for it? When stories hit the news about famous athletes acting in a particularly sportsmanlike or unsportsmanlike fashion, do you discuss these events with your players?

- In what ways do you set a good example for sportsmanlike behavior? In what ways do you set a bad example?

- Do you allow unsportsmanlike behavior in practice that you wouldn't allow in a game? What do you do in practice to help your players develop the *habit* of respect for others and for the game?

Resisting the Temptation to Overcoach

Sometimes the expression "student-centered education," especially at the college level where recruitment and retention of students pay the bills, means giving students whatever they want, as if they are customers of a business or consumers of a product. If consumers want cars with bright colors, who are we to question their judgment? Educating students and manufacturing cars, however, are not the same thing. Respect for the potential of young athletes to learn doesn't mean letting them do whatever they want. It necessarily means making a good many decisions for them, decisions that may not be popular, at least at the time. Otherwise, it makes no sense to say that teachers teach students.

But there is a great danger that we will forget the purpose of making these decisions. Education is an inescapably paternalistic undertaking—that is, it involves teachers making decisions on behalf of students—but it is a paradoxical sort of paternalism. To some extent, it always involves making decisions *for* students, but the purpose of this paternalism is to *educate* them, that is, to bring them to the point at which they can make responsible decisions for themselves. The goal of educational paternalism, like the goal of parental paternalism, is eventually to make itself superfluous.

The tremendous amount of authority that is typically vested in coaches makes it easy for coaches to forget the ultimate goal of this authority. The primary reason for the existence of a scholastic athletic program is the education of young athletes. If you forget that, you can easily come to think that you have this special authority because you're the one who ultimately matters, that the whole team exists for your sake. Then you start to make decisions for the team that will serve your own ends—to advance your own career, to impress local boosters, to inflate your ego. If you do a good job, your career ought to advance, local boosters ought to be impressed, and you should be proud of your accomplishments. It bears mentioning, however, that there is a difference between being proud and being egotistical.

Simply put, the coach can become more important than the players. It's interesting to note the way in which so many of the rule changes of the past few decades, especially in college sports, have made the coach increasingly more important, to the extent that in big-time college athletics the coach often becomes the focus of the whole enterprise. The winning-is-everything attitude very often is related to the overemphasis on the importance of the coach. All too often, for the coach, winning is the sole yardstick of worth. Job, salary, prestige— the win column for the coach has repercussions beyond the playing field. The mirror check on this issue: Am I here for the players, as their coach and teacher—or are they here for me? Am I teaching them or exploiting them?

One of the results of overemphasis on the importance of the coach is the temptation to overcoach. If your record, your career, or your ego becomes the focus of your effort, then it's tempting to make all the decisions for the players, to provide all of the energy and spirit—even if it's the spirit of fear. If your win-loss record is all-important, then you're going to make sure that everything gets done that needs to get done, whether your doing it is in the best interest of the players' education or not. But if you remember that the ultimate purpose is to help your players grow into autonomous adults, at some point you have to let them make the decisions, make the mistakes, make what you've taught them their own. Somewhere along the line, you have to recede as a teacher of the game; you have to fall back into your role as the coach who is an integral part of a team effort; and you have to let them play the game. It is revealing that we talk about the win-loss records of coaches, when in fact, strictly speaking, coaches don't win or lose, teams do. Coaches coach; and, strictly speaking, the players play the game.

TIME-OUT *for Reflection*

- Think of specific examples of ways a coach in your sport can be tempted to overcoach.

- Think of specific ways a coach in your sport can allow players more responsibility. For example, should a scholastic baseball coach call all of the pitches for a catcher and pitcher?

Exhibiting and Teaching the Proper Balance of Playfulness and Seriousness

In effect, then, you demonstrate respect for your players by exhibiting the proper balance of playfulness and seriousness in your own behavior. Coaches who don't take the responsibilities of coaching seriously enough undercoach; coaches who take themselves too seriously, who place too much importance on themselves and not enough on the education of the players, overcoach. Like parents, coaches can err in both directions. You can become so accommodating, like car manufacturers responding to market trends, that you abdicate your responsibility; and you can become so authoritarian that you abuse the legitimate authority vested in you.

In finding this balance, you must be truthful about yourself, specifically, about your own abilities and limitations. Different people will, and should, find different ways of handling the responsibilities of coaching, of showing respect for the players. Some coaches are going to be more playful than others, and some more serious than others. But the basic principle of finding a proper balance is still the goal. During the mirror checks, some coaches need to say "Lighten up," and others, "Get serious."

For those who need to lighten up, one way to gain a perspective on this balance is to view sport in relation to the rest of life, as we'll discuss in chapter 8. To the athletes on the playing field, the game is everything, and seriousness about competition requires that we don't step on the field unless we intend to give it all we've got; but, at the same time, we'd do well to consider the outcome of a high school football game or swimming meet alongside, say, men, women, and children dying in the car bombing of a federal building in Oklahoma City, scientists trying to discover a cure for AIDS, teenagers dying in drive-by shootings in cities all over the nation, and families driven from their homes, tortured, and murdered in the civil war in Bosnia.

It's a game, coach. Sport isn't everything. It's an avenue to some very important things for many people; but there are other avenues.

TIME-OUT *for Reflection*

- In chapter 2, in which we first introduced the notion of a balance between playfulness and seriousness, we asked you a series of questions about what you actually do to promote this balance. What sorts of things could you do that you don't currently do to achieve this balance in yourself and to teach it to your players?

WRAP-UP

The relationship between coach and players is special. Depending on the personalities, the age of the players, and the particular sport, that relationship can take many forms. But what we've tried to argue in this chapter is that the foundation of that relationship must be reciprocal respect. That respect, like the respect for opponents, teammates, and officials, is based on the nature of athletic competition and the role that the coach plays in a team effort. And, because the coach in a scholastic setting is an educator in the broadest sense of the word, the responsibility for building this relationship of respect is even greater.

PART THREE

Thinking About Sport and Life

CHAPTER 8

Beyond Sport

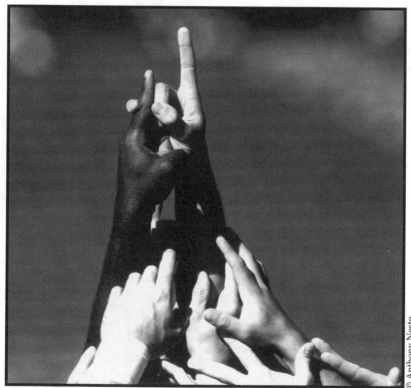

© Anthony Neste

> So, Callicles, I have been convinced by these accounts; it has become my concern how I may present to the judge my soul in its healthiest condition. I relinquish, therefore, the honors that most men pursue and shall endeavor, by cultivating the truth, to be as good as I may during my life and, when I come to die, in my dying. And insofar as I am able I urge all other men (and you in particular I summon, thus countering your former summons to me) to such a life and such a contest as this, which I affirm to be worth all the contests here on earth put together.

—Plato, *The Gorgias (Helmbold translation)*

At the beginning of part I of the book we invited you to become more reflective about your own experience. But becoming more reflective about your own experience inevitably means going beyond your own experience in order to gain perspective on it. In this case, that means thinking about the nature of athletic competition in a more theoretical way than you ordinarily do in the day-to-day activities of an athletic coach. You ought to embody an understanding of the nature of athletic competition when you make split-second decisions during a game or a practice, but you won't be consciously reflecting on it. In order to embody that understanding, however, you do have to think about it, reflect on it, pay attention to what others have thought and said about it. As an educator you do need to set aside time to become more reflective about what you do—and you will do a better job at what you do if you become more reflective about it.

In this part of the book, we invite you to think back on some of the broader themes that we've repeatedly touched on throughout the book and to relate those themes to some of the broader ethical and philosophical issues that we have not dealt with. We invite you to think about the relation between sport and life, or, rather, sport and life as a whole. As we intimated in chapter 2, underlying the two extreme views of sport are equally extreme views about what life is all about. Thinking about sport, just like thinking about any serious human endeavor, leads us inevitably to think about the relation between that endeavor and life as a whole.

What we've said so far makes a lot of sense without these connections, but we'd like to leave you with some final thoughts on the relation between sport and life. In "Putting Sport in Perspective," we'll reiterate one of the recurring themes of the book, the need to recognize that sport is not the whole of life; in "Reconnecting Sport and Life," we'll make some suggestions for understanding how sport is, nonetheless, connected to the whole of life—and even how sport is very much "about" life.

We won't provide a series of answers, but we will try to leave you with a sense of the abiding question of human existence: How ought I to live my life? Becoming reflective about sport ultimately means becoming reflective about life.

We think that parts I and II by themselves can help you understand the principles of sportsmanship that you should embody and teach in your coaching, but here we invite you to go one step further and think about how what you do is related to the most basic human questions.

PUTTING SPORT IN PERSPECTIVE

One of the most important themes that we have developed in this book concerns perspective. Of course, in one obvious sense the only way we can see things is from where we are. But it is a remarkable fact of human experience that we have the capacity to see things so differently *from where we are*. We inevitably use spatial metaphors here. We can see things "narrowly" or "broadly"; we can be "closed-minded" or we can "enlarge" our vision; our point of view can be "cramped" and "limited," but we even have the capacity to consider how things might look from God's perspective, *sub specie aeternitatis*. We are finite beings, spatially and temporally, but our minds roam over infinity. In one context, we think of our true selves as what's "inside"—especially when we talk about feelings and emotions. But, in another context, we lose track of any sense of the "inside," and we focus our attention on something "outside" ourselves—the catcher's mitt, a beautiful mountain, another person. In fact, when we describe our *experience*, it's not at all clear that the concepts of inside and outside make sense at all.

Our perspective on the world is always limited, but it's often broader than we give ourselves credit for; and often it could become broader than our egos would have us believe. Often the only way to understand and appreciate what is closest to us is to cast our glance away from it in order to see it against a wider background. And when we do this, something happens to us. Because we see more broadly, we see more. We compare, we inevitably make judgments, and when we return to the object of our original attention, our focus has been reshaped.

As we have suggested, good sportsmanship requires understanding and practice. When we appreciate the wonderful complexity of sports participation, including the essential roles played by opponents, teammates, coaches, and officials, as well as the rich traditions and customs of the various games, our attitudes are changed, *our spirit is enlarged*. The limited desires of the egoistic self are transformed into the respectful concerns of a more substantial self whose character has developed and whose actions attest to this. By seeing ourselves as part of a greater whole, we are enriched by it. But if it is important to turn our respectful gaze toward our fellow participants *within* the world of sport, it is perhaps even more important, from the standpoint of our fundamental attitudes and the development of character, to turn our reflective attention away from sport to the whole of life. We need perspective on sport itself.

"It's Only a Game"

As we have argued, coaches are moral educators, if not by explicit instruction then at least by the habits they instill and the examples they set. The game, however, has the power not only to uplift and encourage, it can also depress and ultimately destroy—if it is not kept in perspective. Consider the sad case of a former major league pitcher, whose life spiraled downward badly and ended in suicide after he gave up the Big Homer in the playoffs. There is a monumental difference between playing the game *as if* it were the only thing in the world that mattered and truly believing it *is* the only thing in the world that matters. Coaches have a tremendous responsibility in this regard. As motivators they must get their players to play as if each game, each inning, each pitch were indeed the only thing in the universe that mattered; as educators in the broad sense they must figure out how to do this in such a way that they never let their players forget that no pitch, no inning, no game, is—pardon the sports metaphor—the whole ball game. Or, to use the standard expression, "It's only a game."

Perhaps it's a cliché or such an obvious truism that its outward expression seems unneeded, but sometimes wisdom is nothing other than internalizing and living the truth of the truism. And that requires that we think about the truism, for the truth of a truism is not the simple fact that it states, but the perspective it calls for. Truisms ask us to see things in light of something so obvious we often ignore it. "Man cannot live by bread alone," "Everyone must die" . . . "It's only a game." Everybody knows it's only a game, but we need to state the obvious because it's easy to become so absorbed in the game that we forget the obvious. To live the truth of the truism that it's only a game is to come to appreciate how sport fits into the whole of life, where the true value of sport resides, and how to integrate the love of the game and the pursuit of athletic excellence into a life lived well. It means putting sport within the proper perspective and maintaining the proper balance of seriousness and playfulness that a broader perspective calls for. As a coach and an educator you must communicate this truism—not by mindlessly stating it or posting it on the locker-room wall—but with all your actions and all your words.

As we write, and as coaches all over America tell young athletes that winning this game is the only thing that matters, there are children who are living and dying in such abysmal circumstances that they have never had the opportunity to play an organized game of any kind. In a world in which hunger, disease, suffering, and violence confront us daily, the value of devoting our attention to playing athletic games should be affirmed with some degree of modesty. The internal goals of sports—throwing a slow curve ball well, shooting an arrow into the 10 ring at 90 meters in a strong crosswind, hitting a perfect touch volley—seem trivial by comparison. Athletic games can be exuberant, intensely absorbing, joyful, but, at its best, sport is *splendid triviality*. To say that sport is splendid triviality is to acknowledge its modest place in the scale of significant human concerns. Nor is sport the only human practice that offers so much to its participants and fans. Certainly there are other practices—music, art, mathematics—that can be just as demanding, as rich, as educational, and, in their own way, as joyful as sport. Turning our attention away from our immediate concern with sport and toward the whole of life should produce another kind of humility, one which wisely recognizes the smallness of our athletic concerns in the face of the largeness of life. Coaches need to remind players how lucky they are to be able to *play*, to be able to pursue this unique kind of excellence for at least a small part of their lives.

Winners and Losers in Life?

From the standpoint of this broader perspective, some of the facile analogies between sport and life that tend to blow up the athletic arena until it encompasses everything lose their legitimacy. Yes, life is like a baseball game (or, as one of our friends more ironically put it, life is a metaphor for baseball)—but in what respects? Too often the sport-life analogy develops a life of its own, and becomes an answer to every question, a cure for every ill. If we situate sport within the context of the whole of life, we might well "live the truth of the truisms" about sport and life, but there is a corresponding danger that we will let the endless slogans, clichés, and analogies do our thinking for us. Some truisms state the obvious in order to give us perspective; some slogans and analogies overstate the case to make a point; and some slogans and analogies, because of their rhetorical punch, trick us into accepting a view of sport and life that we might otherwise see through.

Two examples: "Winning isn't everything; it's the only thing" and "Show me a good loser and I'll show you a loser." As rhetorical devices designed to get players to walk on the field in order to play *as if* this game is the only thing that matters, to help them avoid the trap of walking on the field prepared to lose, these slogans may serve a legitimate purpose. But all too often we take them, or even consciously intend for them, to mean that, literally, sport and life are about winning and nothing else. Then we end up with school board members claiming that a losing season teaches the players to be "losers in life" or a winning season teaches them to be "winners in life," a claim that misconstrues both the nature of sport and the nature of life. There are indeed winners in sport, but is there really such a thing as a winner in life? If one side wins in sport, the other side necessarily loses. If I am a winner in life, would I then cause someone else to be a loser? That analogy might make sense in the business world—if I make a lot of money, someone else will make less—but if I live the best life I am capable of living, if I am the best person I am capable of being, do I cause others to live worse lives, to be worse human beings? On the contrary, as we have already discussed, my living well—that is, living ethically well—will enhance the lives of those around me.

Of course, when we thought more deeply about the nature of competitive sport, we found that sport, in the end, is not about winning either, but about the mutual striving for excellence. Interestingly enough, John Wooden even resorted to the metaphorical use of winning to say what he thought was truly important in sport: "I believe we have 'won'—that is, accomplished all we're capable of accomplishing—when we've *lost* games," he said (Walton, p. 67). Wooden, having thought deeply about sport and about life, kept the metaphor in its proper place by quickly explaining what he really meant by the word "won." In other words, it isn't really the winning in sport that ought to serve as a model for life, but the excellence we achieve in doing our best to win. The athletic experience can no more be reduced to the winning-is-everything cliché than life can be reduced to looking out for number one in a dog-eat-dog world. Life is about being tough enough to stand up to enemies when we ought to stand up to them, tough enough to walk away when we ought to walk away, and tough enough to cultivate friendships, to contribute to the excellence of others, even occasionally to make friends of enemies. Some have even argued that life requires the moral courage to love our enemies.

RECONNECTING SPORT AND LIFE

Even if sport isn't everything, it's surely something, and if we're right about what we've said in this book, it can be an important thing at that. Sport is separate from the rest of life—it takes place in special places marked off from the rest of the world. But these special places and the games we play in them have more to do with the rest of our lives than this separation might suggest.

The Virtue of Sportsmanship and the Virtues of a Life Lived Well

As we have argued, sport provides an arena in which good character can be developed and practiced. Sport is surely not the only arena in which young people can learn to be persistent, determined, respectful, trustworthy, courageous, responsible, fair, and honest. If young people devote themselves to any practices in which there are standards of excellence, traditions, and learned teachers, such virtues can be developed. Young violinists as well as young gymnasts have an opportunity to practice virtue. But sport is important and pervasive in our lives. In sport we have ample opportunities to help young people become the kind of people who will not only be successful and respected in the world of sport, but in life as well. And even the more mature members of the sport world—coaches, administrators, and parents—will have significant and unique moral challenges to confront as they respond to the tensions and dramatic resonances of competitive athletics. Sport may not be everything, but it can have real existential bite.

Sport and life are connected, not because there are winners and losers in life, but because good character matters in both. Aristotle described the goal of a human life this way: "We reach the conclusion that the good of man is an activity of the soul in conformity with excellence or virtue, and if there are several virtues, with the best and most complete" (Aristotle, p. 17). In that sense, moral education in athletics—that is, education in excellence of character—can prepare young people for life. Courage, discipline, fairness—simply put, these are good things.

Sport and the Virtues of the Mind

Our extended comments on sport and character in this book have hardly exhausted the subject. We have articulated and defended various principles of sportsmanship, but our comments have also served to raise important questions. We are convinced that questions about sport and character should be raised by all coaches, in order to promote reflection on the part of the players. To make the right choices in light of principles of sportsmanship requires experience and good judgment. It may be obvious to most thoughtful people that sport can promote the growth of certain character traits. In particular, sport can emphasize virtues of character like courage and responsibility. But what about the traits that will come into play when athletes—and especially coaches and administrators—have to address fundamental questions about what they are doing, how they are to act, and how they stand in relation to life as a whole? It's not at all clear that sport, in and of itself, promotes the intellectual virtues of critical thinking. Sport is competitive *physical* play. Yet moral education in the full sense of the word is not mindless moral indoctrination or even the unreflective inculcation of values. Moral wisdom requires experience, deliberation, and good judgment. Moral education in its full sense requires the development of good thinking along with good character, a good head along with a good heart.

So why shouldn't you ask questions and invite players to *reflect*, not simply to be obedient? Why shouldn't you challenge players to question themselves? Why shouldn't you show players that it is important to thoughtfully engage in sport? As participating athletes we all yearn for the "unconsciousness" of a great streak, but as full human beings, we should aspire to the kind of thoughtful reflection that enables us to *understand* why the experience of a streak is so uplifting, what it means to say it is "unconscious," and why this sort of experience has to be situated within a whole life lived well. Socratic questioning is generally inappropriate in the middle of a basketball game (although Socratic irony might sometimes be advisable in disagreeing with an official), but there is no reason that coaches and teachers can't teach student athletes to reflect—at least after the game is over—about the meaning of their experiences on the court or playing field. In other words, in order to make the connection between sport and life meaningful, we may need to cultivate virtues of the mind that athletic experience itself may not naturally promote.

Sport: Escape or Revelation?

When we start to *think* about sport, we recognize that character development does not exhaust the meaning that sport has for us. We have repeatedly referred to the exhilaration, the beauty, of the game. Indeed, there may be a further relation between sport and life that bears some thought. Or is there? Some critics, and even some defenders, claim that sport is an escape from the realities of everyday life. The critics say it is a delusionary escape from real life; the defenders say it takes us away from the injustice and toil of the work world, that it creates an ideal space in which the good triumph and the bad lose. There's probably some truth in both of these views: Sport does create a separate world, take us out of the everyday, the ordinary, the workaday. It has a beauty all its own. The exhilaration, then, seems to come, not from a connection between sport and life, but from their separateness.

But the separateness of our fields of dreams, like the separateness of our actual dreams, can be misleading. One doesn't have to accept the full-blown apparatus of Freudian psychoanalysis to recognize that dreams often reflect the deeper concerns of our waking lives. Perhaps a better analogy—one which is not commonly made—might be between sport and art. We speak of the art world much as we speak of the sports world—the world of art is a world of its own, and the works of art produced in it create their own worlds. Works of art are creations out of nothing, fictions, products of the imagination. In fact, many philosophers have identified art as a form of play.

But this characterization can be misleading. For great art, and even not-so-great art, takes us out of the everyday, the ordinary, creates a separate world of its own—but ultimately reflects back upon the whole of life. We come away from an inspired performance of a Bach concerto, a made-up arrangement of sounds, with a sense of transcendence, a sense of how the harmony of seemingly discordant strands is at the heart of all things. We come away from Faulkner's fictitious Yoknapatawpha County with a sense of the power of past and place, a deeper sense of what it means to be human. We come away from van Gogh's swirling distortions in *Starry Night* with a deeper understanding of the emotions we all feel in the face of the swirling vastness of the universe. The separateness of an artwork opens up a special space in which we come to see things about ourselves and the world that we could not otherwise see. On one level, art appears to be an escape from reality; on another, it reveals it, reflects it, even enriches it. The purpose of dramatic "playing," says Hamlet, "both at the first and now, was and is, to hold, as 'twere, the mirror up to nature, to show virtue her own feature, scorn her own image, and the very age and body of the time his form and pressure" (III. ii).

We suggest that sport, like art, holds so much meaning for us because, at some deeper level that is difficult to articulate, it too reflects back on the whole of life. If we're thoughtful in how we teach particular sports, if we're dedicated and conscientious, and if we're graced with good luck, we may have experiences in sport that put us in touch with some of the deeper realities of life. Sport, like art, may appear to be a mere escape from reality—and, let's be honest, it very often does function as just that—but it can provide a special mirror for it, a stage for its presentation, an open space in which some very important things can show themselves.

From this perspective, it may well be possible to raise again the notion that life is a kind of game, or at least a form of play. As an invitation to pursue some of these questions and to use athletic experience as a springboard for this reflection, we'll mention a few of the thoughts on this subject that we've developed more fully elsewhere. The view you hold of life—for example, do you think of life as fundamentally a matter of work or play?—will affect the view you have of sport. If life is fundamentally work, then play isn't an opportunity for revelation, but rather a mere escape from the reality of work. But, by the same token, the experiences we have in playing seriously may well reflect on how we view life. The anthropologist Johan Huizinga suggests that humans are essentially *playing* creatures, and more than one philosopher has suggested that life might well be understood as dead-serious play. It's reasonable to say that life ought to be lived as if it mattered absolutely, even though in some ultimate sense none of us knows if it really matters. Of course, the *as-if* quality of a ball game comes in part from the fact that we know there will be other games and other experiences in life, whereas we have only one life to live. The as-if quality of the play of life, then, has a different character. On the one hand, when we say that someone treats life as a game, or is playing at life, we mean to say that this person doesn't take it seriously enough. On the other hand, we often need to remind others or ourselves to lighten up, to keep a sense of humor, to appreciate the ironic character of life. Is the balance of playfulness and seriousness we articulated in our discussion of sport the same balance we ought to seek in life?

It's worth mentioning here that thinking about the nature of play has even led some philosophers and theologians not merely beyond the ballpark and the art gallery, but even beyond the questions about the place of play in a human life. We can and often do draw facile, self-serving analogies between sport and life, and as we broaden the spheres of play, the possibility of making connections too quickly and too easily increases. Nonetheless, if we think about sport as a form of play, that is, as an activity that has no purpose beyond itself, we might well come to wonder not just whether human life is in some fundamental sense a matter of play, but whether reality in general doesn't have something of this character. Friedrich Schlegel wrote: "All the sacred games of art are only remote imitations of the infinite play of the world, the eternally self-creating work of art" (Gadamer, p. 101). Isn't it possible to ask the same question about the sacred games of sport?

If play is a purely human phenomenon, something we make up, then all of the other references we make to play—the play of waves in the ocean, the wind playing tricks with us, the play of light on the water, the "infinite play of the world"—would be metaphorical. Those things don't *really*, literally play—we simply see them in light of human experience. Some thinkers, however, have suggested that the self-renewal of nature, its effortless playing of itself without any purpose beyond itself, might well be the "literal" sense of play. That play feels so "natural" to us might well come from deeper sources in us than we realize. Play, then, far from being an escape from reality may be an expression of it. Of course, we don't ordinarily think about these things as we are playing sports, but it may well be that it is precisely because of these deeper connections that we feel, in a way that's difficult to articulate, most "real" when we play.

WRAP-UP

While all of the other chapters of this book achieve some kind of closure, we mean for this chapter to open out into, to point to, what we haven't fully discussed. Underlying the closure of the previous chapters is an arena and a tradition of philosophical reflection that we have only touched upon here, and we hope that these musings might serve as an invitation to spend more time in this "arena." The charge of juvenile escapism has been leveled at philosophy as well—and sometimes with good reason—but we contend that the step back of good thinking, like the seeming artificiality of art and sport, can ultimately put us in touch with the things that truly matter. And when Socrates said the unexamined life is not worth living for a human being, he did not exclude coaches or athletes.

Suggestions for Teaching Sportsmanship

Throughout the book we've punctuated our discussions of the principles of sportsmanship with questions about how you might go about teaching and promoting these principles in your coaching. In the end, as we have stressed, the application of these principles to your day-to-day coaching is something you will have to do for yourself. The application of principles requires good judgment, and you're the one who has to develop and exercise that judgment. Nonetheless, we thought it might be helpful to provide some suggestions for how you might go about putting these principles into practice.

Throughout this book we think we have offered something that is largely missing from our contemporary sport culture: an articulation of the principles of sportsmanship that is grounded in an understanding of the nature of sport. Here, based on our experience as coaches, athletes, and fans—as "students of the game" with regard to at least a few sports—we will throw out some ideas for how an understanding of these principles might show up in the practice of coaching. Let's say you agree that teaching young athletes to respect opponents is an essential part of your responsibilities as a coach. What, then, can you do when you walk onto the practice field or court, when you talk to players before or during or after a game, to fulfill that responsibility?

In chapter 7 we argue that one of the principles of sportsmanship is the respect between players and the coach. The coach must demand respect, and the players owe respect to the coach. But the coach who merely demands respect won't get it. You have to earn it, deserve it, by virtue of the respect you show to your players. One of the coach's obligations toward the players is to exhibit and to teach them the principles of sportsmanship. We included three approaches to the teaching of sportsmanship: (1) teaching by explicit instruction, (2) teaching by example, and (3) practicing sportsmanship. How much you depend on explicit instruction and how much you depend on having your players practice sportsmanship is a function of the age of the players (the older they are the more you can explicitly explain to them) and your own abilities and personality. Regardless of your personality, as you try to get players to form the habit of sportsmanship, you'll have to depend on a variety of approaches. The most obvious device is the use of rules and punishments for the violation of rules. But remember that respect for others, the cornerstone of sportsmanlike behavior, requires first and foremost the *perspective* to see things from the other's point of view. And many of the activities that promote the habit and perspective of sportsmanship—say, the postgame handshake—are not activities required by rules, but by custom and tradition. They take on the character of meaningful rituals that become as much a part of the sport as the rules. Remember that you can develop, even invent, rituals that can become a part of the sport—or at least a part of your team's identity.

First we'll offer a series of general guidelines for teaching sportsmanship to young athletes. These guidelines would apply to any sport that you might coach within a scholastic setting. Then, to illustrate how these guidelines might be applied to a particular sport, we'll offer concrete suggestions for one of the sports we've coached.

GUIDELINES FOR TEACHING SPORTSMANSHIP

1. Be a good role model.   As a coach you must constantly keep in mind that your actions do, in fact, speak louder than your words. No matter what you say, what you do will have an effect on your players. You must do everything you can to show your players what it means to be a good sport by treating opposing players and coaches, officials, team members, and the sport in which you participate with respect. An obvious corollary: Admit to your players when you fall short of your own sportsmanship ideals.

2. Emphasize sportsmanship from the beginning.   The process of "coaching for character" should start early, from your first contact with players. If you're recruiting a player to come out for the team or a player comes to you to discuss trying out, what you say will set the tone for your relationship with that player. At the first team meeting with your players you should explain how much you value sportsmanship. Tell them what your expectations are, how you understand the basic principles of sportsmanship, and why these principles are important.

3. Talk about combining seriousness and playfulness.   Since the principles of sportsmanship are based on the very nature of sport, and sport is a form of competitive play, explain to your players that sport is "serious fun." Help them understand that bad sportsmanship is often a matter of being "too serious," of forgetting that there's more sport than winning, and, in some cases, a matter of not being serious enough, of forgetting that striving to be excellent and striving to win within the rules and customs of the game are essential parts of competition. Try to show this balance in your own attitude and in your comments. Be serious when it's called for; cut up, kid around, and have fun when it's called for. How you express this balance will in part depend on your own personality, but the need for a balance between playfulness and seriousness is not a matter of personal preference or personality. It comes from the nature of the activity you're engaging in, competitive play. Take your responsibilities seriously, but don't take yourself too seriously.

4. Talk about the relationship between sportsmanship and success. Make sure your players understand that "success" in sports is not merely a matter of achieving victory, and that victory without sportsmanship, dignity, and honor is hollow. At the same time, try to show your players that respect for the team and your sport, as well as respect between the players and the coach, might help develop habits and talents that will improve your chances of winning.

5. Regularly use the language of sportsmanship. The language of sportsmanship should become a regular part of your coaching vocabulary. Don't leave this language behind after the first team meeting. The language of "respect" should be heard by your players often. If you earn their respect, the language you use around them will become a part of their way of looking at things. Never underestimate the power of language. The right words make it possible to understand things we couldn't otherwise understand.

6. Expect sportsmanship in practice as well as in games. Since we are encouraging you to develop the habits of good sportsmanship in your players, don't reserve instruction for games only. Expect good behavior—the habit of showing respect—in practice.

7. Establish team rules, customs, rituals, and traditions that reinforce the principles of sportsmanship. While it is crucial to talk about the basic principles of sportsmanship, it is probably even more important to be specific about your expectations. Establish specific team rules that promote good sportsmanship. It's a good idea to list the rules and place them in the context of the principles of sportsmanship. If you demand 100 percent effort at all times, then explain this demand with reference to respecting your opponents, your teammates, and the game. As much as possible, be specific about how you expect your players to relate to opponents, officials, and each other.

When the opportunity arises, try to develop customs, rituals, and traditions that will promote sportsmanship. Some customs and rituals you can simply demand, like the postgame handshake. Others develop out of the special relations and situations; some of them the players develop on their own. Take advantage of those developments.

8. Encourage players to take the perspective of other participants in sports. Since sportsmanship demands proper *perspective*, help players to understand and imaginatively to appreciate others' points of view. This is analogous to the moral education of a child, when a parent sometimes says something like, "How would it make you feel if someone did that to you?" Talk about the "silver rule." Talk about how opponents and officials might look at you and your players.

9. Develop clear guidelines for dealing with unsportsmanlike behavior. Make it clear to your players from the beginning of the season how you will deal with actions that violate the principles of sportsmanship. If you decide not to allow taunting, showboating, or arguing with officials, tell the players what the specific penalty (or gradations of penalties) will be if the rules are violated. You can spell out the sequence of possible punishments and explain that you will decide how serious the violation has been— in other words, you don't have to decide in advance what the penalty for every possible violation will be—but you do have to be clear that there are consequences for violations. Be clear about the process. If you'll make the decisions, say that. If you'll allow the team to be involved, say that.

10. Reinforce good sportsmanship. If good sportsmanship matters to you, show the players, parents, and fans it matters by rewarding good behavior in some manner. The most obvious way to do this is through praise, respectful behavior, and playing time. At the end of the season, make sure that team awards include sportsmanship, either as a separate award or as a necessary condition for all awards.

11. Communicate the importance of sportsmanship to parents. Before the season starts meet with parents and explain to them the value you place on sportsmanship. Enlist their help and support in reinforcing your expectations with their children.

12. Communicate the importance of sportsmanship to fans. Depending on the situation in which you coach, some kind of public announcement concerning sportsmanship is important. You might address this issue over the public address system at a game, or in a printed handout. You can encourage your school or league officials to adopt rules concerning the misbehavior of fans at home games or matches. Try to develop an educational campaign at your school or in your league or organization promoting the ideals of sportsmanship among fans. Rituals at the beginning of a game showing respect for the opponents can help set the tone for the fans. Your remarks at social functions, postgame interviews on the radio, and so on can also set the tone.

13. Talk about news stories concerning sportsmanship with your players. Since most of your players are probably sports fans, use current sporting events as an opportunity for discussing sportsmanship with them. When a famous athlete does something controversial or especially laudable, ask your players what they think about the event. Ask them what they would do if they were the coach. Discuss with them how you would deal with that sort of behavior. To some extent, you can help them to see which famous athletes deserve our respect and which do not.

14. Talk about specific incidents with your players. Encourage your players to bring up incidents that happen to them in sports. Take advantage of things that come up to discuss sportsmanship with your players.

15. Promote reflectiveness by asking questions. Remember that you are a teacher and that good teaching often involves asking the right questions, rather than giving the students carefully packaged answers. Encourage players to think for themselves and make their own reasoned judgments about their experiences or examples you call attention to.

16. Talk about the history of your sport with players. Talk with your athletes about the historical traditions, innovations, and heroes of your sport in order to broaden their perspective and enrich their sense of participating in something bigger than themselves. Tell good stories. Encourage players to read about the history of their sport in order to develop a respect for the fullness of the game.

17. Expect players to know the rule book. To encourage players to respect the game as well as the officials, encourage them to study the rule book. Ask them questions about the interpretation of difficult situations if they were officiating. Play "You make the call."

18. Show by your actions and your words that you care, that what you're trying to teach is important. No matter how much your players may seem to resist you, many of your values will become theirs. Let them know that it matters how they behave, what kind of human beings they will be, whether they do things well or poorly.

19. Don't forget to have fun. Remember it's a game. It's serious, it matters, but it's play. Show your players that what they're doing matters, but don't take yourself too seriously. If no one is having fun, you're not playing a game anymore.

AN EXAMPLE OF TEACHING SPORTSMANSHIP: BASEBALL

It would be impossible to list specific suggestions for teaching sportsmanship in every possible sport in which a young person might participate, but it might be helpful, as a model, to offer suggestions for one particular sport. Of course, there are decisions you must make as coach about how to apply the principles of sportsmanship that will not be encompassed by a rule, custom, or tradition—or by any suggestion we might make here. That's why we've emphasized the concept of good judgment throughout the book. But a few concrete examples of how we've emphasized the various principles of sportsmanship in coaching a particular sport might make the principles more meaningful for you. These suggestions are not meant to be exhaustive, but they are extensive and specific enough to give you an idea of how you might apply the principles of sportsmanship.

Suppose you are coaching a youth-league or high school baseball team. Here are some things that we've found useful in teaching good sportsmanship to young baseball players. Some of them are based on long-standing tradition, and some we've come up with based on our own experiences.

Respect for Opponents

(a) Don't allow your players to yell at opponents from the dugout.

(b) Teach your players that it's all right to cheer when your teammates do something good but not when your opponents make errors or can't throw strikes.

(c) Have your players shake hands meaningfully after the game. Win or lose, they should take this ritual seriously.

(d) If you lose, you and your players should offer sincere congratulations after the game. To show they mean it, they should praise the opponent in a specific manner (e.g., "Way to hit the ball!").

(e) Treat the opposing coach with respect and demand that your players do the same.

(f) Don't allow players to act cocky.

(g) Don't allow players to change their attitude or approach to the game whether you're winning or losing. If you're winning, don't allow them to get "chirpy." That is, don't allow them to start laughing and making wisecracks. The same goes for the coach.

(h) After an away game be sure to have your team clean the dugout.

(i) Insist that players avoid displays of emotional immaturity when they strike out, make an error, and so on.

(j) In postgame discussions, especially with opponents, don't whine or make excuses, and don't allow your players to whine or make excuses. Insist that they accept defeat gracefully, acknowledging their opponents' excellence.

(k) If you're winning by a large margin in late innings, don't run up the score. You can't ask your players not to swing at the ball or to quit playing good baseball (which would be insulting to the opposing team in its own way), but you can abide by the customs of the game that apply to this situation. Don't hit and run, try to steal bases, and so on.

Respect for Teammates and Team

(a) Require your players to concentrate on the game. Every team member should know the score, inning, and count at every moment in the game.

(b) Teach players to support their teammates. They should yell for them at appropriate moments. Players should congratulate teammates for doing things well, especially "little things." If a player successfully sacrifices a runner into scoring position, the entire team should get off the bench and congratulate the player when he or she returns to the dugout.

(c) Don't allow parents or friends near the dugout during the game. Players should talk only to members of the team during the game. Allowing the interference or involvement of parents during a game will break down the unity of the team.

(d) During the game players should talk to each other only about the game.

(e) Players should be allowed to leave the dugout only for game-related reasons or for emergencies. Every player is part of the team effort to win the game.

(f) Insist that every player help his or her teammates become better in practice. Every member of the team should be willing to throw batting practice, hit fungoes, work with younger players, and so on.

(g) If possible, require players to travel together to and from away games.

(h) Never allow young players to seek advice or instruction from their parents, relatives, or friends *during* practice or games.

(i) Expect all players to conform to the same team rules and customs. The quickest way to destroy team unity is to play favorites when applying rules.

Respect for Officials

(a) Players should address umpires in a formal manner (e.g., "Mr. or Ms. Umpire," "Sir," or "Ma'am").

(b) Insist that players be polite or civil when talking to an umpire.

(c) Don't allow players to argue with umpires—the coach should address the situation.

(d) Shake hands with the umpires after the game.

(e) Congratulate the umpire if you think the game was officiated well. (Apologize if you lost your cool during the game, and have your players apologize if they did.)

(f) After the game don't allow players to blame umpires for a loss. Stress the idea that acceptance of the human judgment of umpires is part of the game.

(g) Talk with players about umpires, especially those who are good. Help players appreciate excellence in umpiring by praising good umpires. Perhaps require your players, depending on their age, to umpire lower level competition so that they will learn to the see the game from an umpire's perspective.

(h) Teach your players the cardinal rule of respect for officials in baseball: Don't show up the umpire! Teach them the customs of the game regarding behavior toward umpires, for example, catchers holding a missed call way beyond catching it, catchers or batters turning around toward the umpire to disagree with a call, and so on.

Respect for the Game

(a) Teach your players the cardinal rule of respect for the game: Play hard! All the time, ahead or behind, early inning or late inning. That means they should run out every ball, back up teammates on throws, and so on.

(b) Players should hustle on and off the field. Explain to them that this shows enthusiasm for the game.

(c) Require players to wear their uniform in an appropriate manner. For example, a cap should not be worn backwards in a game or in practice.

(d) Expect your players to learn the nuances of the game. Teach them about the game. Ask them questions about strategy.

(e) Respect rules. Don't break them yourself and don't allow players to break them. For example, make sure all equipment (bats, balls, gloves, etc.) is legal. Explain to your team that breaking the rules means you're not playing the game.

(f) Help players understand and abide by the traditions and customs of the game. For example, don't allow players to steal bases, hit and run, squeeze, and so on, when your team is beating an opponent badly. Running up the score is clearly disrespectful to the opponent, but it also shows that you don't respect the game you're playing enough to abide by its customs.

(g) Talk about and promote the heroes and innovators of the game. Tell good stories about them.

(h) Talk about the history of the game. Insist that players study the history of the game. (You might emphasize this point by having baseball history quizzes on the van during road trips.)

(i) Require all players to *act* like they love the game. For example, don't allow players to act "cool," as if they are above the game. Explain to them that acting cool is nothing but a way of protecting yourself against the disappointment of defeat. It hurts more to lose if you've given your best and acted as if you cared, but there is no other acceptable way to play the game.

(j) Attempt to instill in players a sense of being *thankful* for the opportunity to play the game. Remind them that a lot of people have gone to a great deal of trouble and expense to make it possible for them to play the game.

Respect Between Players and Coach

(a) Tell the players specifically how they may address you. "Coach" is highly recommended; calling you by your first name is not. It shows their acceptance of your role, and, of course, it commits you to live up to being their coach.

(b) Expect players to listen carefully to your instructions. In team meetings, don't allow players to talk while the coach is talking.

(c) Be clear about who makes the various decisions on the team. It is the coach, for example, who fills out the lineup card, not the players, parents, or fans.

(d) Use an appropriate model or analogy to explain how you understand your authority and the responsibilities of the players. For example, you might suggest that your players treat you as they would a parent or a respected teacher.

(e) Be specific about little signs of disrespect that will not be tolerated: eyes rolling, moping, lack of hustle, questioning decisions at inappropriate times, and so on.

(f) Show players that you respect them by expecting mature behavior from them and by treating them, as much as possible, as adults who are capable of understanding your and their roles on the team.

(g) Reserve some time during the season to talk to each player individually. Talk about how the player thinks things are going on the team. Ask for suggestions, and discuss them.

(h) Exhibit the principles of sportsmanship in your own behavior, and teach them the principles of sportsmanship through example and explicit instruction and by developing practice routines that instill the character traits of sportsmanship.

(i) Don't forget that your players need to have fun. Reserve some practice time for drills or activities that are strictly for fun.

Bibliography

In order not to break up the text unnecessarily, we have avoided the mechanisms of scholarly citation as much as possible. We have, however, depended heavily on certain sources, in some cases directly quoting and in others not, so it is appropriate to give credit where credit is due.

Secondly, we would like to give some indication of the background that informs this book. The conciseness and clarity we've achieved in articulating the principles of sportsmanship derive in part from our experience as coaches and athletes, but in large part from our philosophical backgrounds. Some of these sources we refer to explicitly in the text of our book, and others are listed here because they have informed our thinking in a significant way.

Finally, in the event that someone might want to pursue some of these topics in a more scholarly fashion, we wanted to use this opportunity to suggest additional readings.

For these reasons our list of bibliographical entries is preceded by a short bibliographical essay explaining the most significant sources that have informed our thinking on the subject of sportsmanship. We will first say a few words about some of the more significant influences on our thinking; then we'll provide a more complete list of relevant readings and sources.

Our view of sport as a form of play has been influenced by various writers. *Homo Ludens: A Study of the Play Element in Culture* by Johan Huizinga is perhaps *the* seminal study of play and its relation to various expressions of human culture—language, law, war, poetry, and so on. The first chapter contains an important analysis of the concept of play. Kenneth Schmitz's "Sport and Play: Suspension of the Ordinary" is one of the most concise applications of Huizinga's concept of play to the arena of sport, and our treatment of the nature of sport in chapter 2 follows his thinking very closely.

In *Truth and Method*, the great German philosopher Hans-Georg Gadamer puts forward the view that art is a form of play. Although he only briefly discusses sport and games, his account helps to clarify the way in which both art and sport are forms of a fundamental aspect of being human, perhaps even a fundamental aspect of nature. We touch briefly on this broader approach to the concept of play in chapter 8.

For obvious reasons, our emphasis on achieving a balance between playfulness and seriousness in sport and sportsmanship closely follows Randolph Feezell's essays "Play and the Absurd" and "Sportsmanship."

Craig Clifford's "Coach" treats many of the ideas that we've developed here in the form of a dialogue, and, for obvious reasons, our "Coach Skeptical" device was modeled on some of the passages in this dialogue.

Our view of competition has been strongly influenced by Drew Hyland's account in his article "Competition and Friendship" and in chapter 2 of his book, *Philosophy of Sport*. The idea that competition is a "mutual striving for excellence" we take from Hyland.

Another great German philosopher, Martin Heidegger (Gadamer's teacher), has been a significant influence. His book *Being and Time* contains one of the most profound reflections on the nature of human existence in the history of philosophy. In particular, our emphasis on understanding human finitude derives in large part from Heidegger's thought. His understanding of human "authenticity" in terms of seeing one's true possibilities is particularly pertinent. Iris Murdoch's essay "The Sovereignty of Good Over Other Concepts" parallels Heidegger's call for a truthful coming to terms with our own finitude. Murdoch connects the development of virtue, or moral excellence, with coming to see the world as it is; that is, she relates the possibility of making ourselves better with a kind of truthful vision of the world, what she calls attaining a "just mode of vision." She also interprets humility in terms of "seeing the way things are." This concept is crucial to our understanding of sportsmanship, and we make reference to it throughout the book.

Our treatment of virtue as excellence of character is, of course, indebted to the classical Greek tradition of moral philosophy, expressed most profoundly in many of Plato's dialogues and in Aristotle's *Nichomachean Ethics*. The role of good judgment (*phronēsis*) in relation to the development of good character is famously emphasized by Aristotle in Book VI of his *Ethics*. Randolph Feezell's "Sport, Character, and Virtue" shows the way in which various virtues might be developed through participation in sports. Feezell's essay and, in general, our understanding of the relation between virtue and sport are heavily influenced by Alasdair MacIntyre's widely discussed book, *After Virtue*. This important work in moral philosophy first situates the virtues in the context of what MacIntyre calls "practices." One distinguishing characteristic of a practice, according to MacIntyre, is that it is a human activity that involves standards of excellence. You can do it well or poorly. Baseball or football or any sport would be a practice; so would playing the violin. MacIntyre distinguishes the internal goods of a practice (in baseball that would include hitting a good line drive) from the external goods that participation in a practice may bring about (fame and fortune, for example). He emphasizes that the internal goods are in some sense shared by participants in the practice (hitting a forehand with more topspin after seeing Bjorn Borg play), unlike the external goods that are in principle scarce (fame and fortune).

Also, our emphasis on the historical nature of sport follows MacIntyre's emphasis on the way practices are constituted by their traditions. A more in-depth account of our thinking about the importance of custom and tradition for understanding the issue of cheating in sports is found in Randolph Feezell's "On the Wrongness of Cheating and Why Cheaters Can't Play the Game." In this essay, cheating is understood as taking an unfair advantage of an opponent. It might involve violating explicit rules, but it might also be a matter of failing to respect the customs and traditions that all participants of the game have implicitly agreed to abide by.

Our view of the function of rules and the role of officials is, not surprisingly, described in the familiar language of Thomas Hobbes. In chapter XIII of *Leviathan*, Hobbes describes a hypothetical situation, which he calls the "state of war," in which people live prior to the development of moral constraints. We've found his description of the state of war helpful in trying to understand what sports would become after the dissolution of moral constraints— assuming, for the purposes of argument, that that has not already occurred.

In chapter 6 of *The Culture of Narcissism*, Christopher Lasch provides an interesting commentary on the "Degradation of Sport" and the trivialization of sport and athletics in contemporary culture. He speaks of sport as "splendid futility." Since he emphasizes the playful character of sport, he might well have agreed with our characterization of sport as "splendid triviality."

Finally, our comments on wisdom and truisms have been influenced by Stanley Godlovitch's essay, "On Wisdom."

Aristotle. *Nichomachean Ethics.* Translated by Martin Ostwald. Indianapolis: Bobbs-Merrill (Library of Liberal Arts), 1962.

Bennett, William J. *The Book of Virtues: A Treasury of Great Moral Stories.* New York: Simon and Schuster, 1993.

Bradley, Bill. *Life on the Run.* New York: Vintage Books, 1976.

Clifford, Craig. "Coach." *The Tenure of Phil Wisdom: Dialogues.* University Press of American, 1995.

Clifford, Craig. "Temper-Tantruming: The Immoral Implications of Tennis." *Fort Worth Star-Telegram,* 22 July 1985 (also appeared in *Baltimore Sun,* 11 August 1985).

Clifford, Craig. "Whatever the Goal in Life or Sports, Winning Is More Than Highest Score." *Fort Worth Star-Telegram,* 3 April 1988 (also appeared in *San Diego Tribune,* 8 April 1988).

Feezell, Randolph. "On the Wrongness of Cheating and Why Cheaters Can't Play the Game." *Journal of the Philosophy of Sport* 15 (January 1988).

Feezell, Randolph. "Play and the Absurd." *Philosophy Today* 28, no. 4 (winter 1984).

Feezell, Randolph. "Play, Freedom, and Sport." *Philosophy Today* 25, no. 2 (summer 1981).

Feezell, Randolph. "Sport, Character, and Virtue." *Philosophy Today* 33, no. 3 (fall 1989).

Feezell, Randolph. "Sportsmanship." *Journal of the Philosophy of Sport* 13 (1986).

Feezell, Randolph, and Curtis L. Hancock. *How Should I Live? Philosophical Conversations about Moral Life.* New York: Paragon House, 1991.

Ford, Gerald. "In Defense of the Competitive Urge." *Sport Inside Out: Readings in Literature and Philosophy.* Edited by David L. Vanderwerden and Spencer K. Wertz. Fort Worth: Texas Christian University Press, 1985.

Gadamer, Hans-Georg. *Truth and Method*. Translated by Joel Weinsheimer and Donald G. Marshall. New York: Continuum, 1993.

Godlovitch, Stanley. "On Wisdom." *Canadian Journal of Philosophy* (March 1981).

Heidegger, Martin. *Being and Time*. Translated by John Macquarrie and Edward Robinson. New York: Harper and Row, 1962.

Heinegg, Peter. "Philosopher in the Playground: Notes on the Meaning of Sport." *Sport Inside Out: Readings in Literature and Philosophy*. Edited by David L. Vanderwerden and Spencer K. Wertz. Fort Worth: Texas Christian University Press, 1985.

Herrigel, Eugen. *Zen in the Art of Archery*. Translated by R.R.C. Hull. New York: Vintage Books, 1971.

Hobbes, Thomas. *Leviathan*. Selections in *Classics of Western Philosophy*, 4th edition. Edited by Steven M. Cahn. Indianapolis: Hackett Publishing Co., 1995.

Huizinga, Johan. *Homo Ludens: A Study of the Play-Element in Culture*. Boston: Beacon Press, 1950.

Hyland, Drew A. "Competition and Friendship," *Journal of the Philosophy of Sport* V (1978).

Hyland, Drew A. *Philosophy of Sport*. New York: Paragon House, 1990.

Jackson, Phil. *Sacred Hoops*. New York: Hyperion, 1995.

Kant, Immanuel. *Grounding for the Metaphysics of Morals*. Translated by James Ellington. Indianapolis: Hackett, 1981.

Lasch, Christopher. *The Culture of Narcissism: American Life in an Age of Diminished Expectations*. New York: Warner Books, 1979.

Lipsyte, Robert. "The Emasculation of American Sports." *The New York Times Magazine* (April 2, 1995).

MacIntyre, Alasdair. *After Virtue: A Study in Moral Theory*. Notre Dame: University of Notre Dame Press, 1981.

Maclean, Norman. *A River Runs Through It and Other Stories*. Chicago: University of Chicago Press, 1976.

Morgan, William J., and Klaus V. Meier. *Philosophic Inquiry in Sport*. Champaign, IL: Human Kinetics, 1988.

Murdoch, Iris. "The Sovereignty of Good Over Other Concepts." *The Sovereignty of Good*. New York: Schocken Books, 1971.

Plato. *The Collected Works of Plato*. Edited by Edith Hamilton and Huntington Cairns. Princeton: Princeton University Press, 1961.

Plato. *The Gorgias*. Translated by W.C. Helmbold. Indianapolis: Library of Liberal Arts (Bobbs-Merrill), 1952.

Plato. *The Republic*. Translated by Benjamin Jowett. New York: Vintage Books, 1991.

Roberts, Randy, and James S. Olson. *Winning Is the Only Thing: Sports in America Since 1945*. Baltimore: Johns Hopkins University Press, 1989.

Schmitz, Kenneth. "Sport and Play: Suspension of the Ordinary." *Philosophic Inquiry in Sport*. Champaign, IL: Human Kinetics, 1988.

Verducci, Tom. "Baseball's Best." *Sports Illustrated* (May 1, 1995).

Walton, Gary M. *Beyond Winning: The Timeless Wisdom of Great Philosopher Coaches*. Champaign, IL: Leisure Press, 1992.

Will, George F. *Men at Work: The Craft of Baseball*. New York: HarperCollins, 1990.

About the Authors

Craig Clifford is associate professor of philosophy at Tarleton State University in Stephenville, Texas. He also is director of the honors programs at Tarleton State.

Clifford received a PhD in philosophy from the State University of New York at Buffalo in 1981. He has an extensive background teaching ethics and philosophy of sport, both at the undergraduate and graduate level.

A frequent author on the subject of sportsmanship, Clifford has published more than one hundred guest columns in major newspapers. He is also the author of *The Tenure of Phil Wisdom: Dialogues* (University Press of America, 1995) and *In the Deep Heart's Core: Reflections on Life, Letters, and Texas* (Texas A&M University Press, 1985).

From 1988 to 1992, Clifford was the head varsity men's and women's tennis coach at Tarleton. During that time, Tarleton qualified three times for the NAIA national tournament.

Recently, Clifford has taken up the sport of Olympic-style target archery. In 1996, his second year of competition, he finished the year ranked third in the state of Texas. He is an active member of the Texas State Archery Association and the National Archery Association.

Randolph M. Feezell is professor of philosophy at Creighton University in Omaha, Nebraska.

Feezell played college baseball at the University of Oklahoma. He has coached baseball at all levels, from Little League to American Legion to college, including experience as an assistant coach at Dana College in Blair, Nebraska.

The author of numerous articles on the philosophy of sport and ethics, Feezell is the coauthor, with Curtis Hancock, of *How Should I Live? Philosophical Conversations About Moral Life* (Paragon House, 1991). He also is the author of *Faith, Freedom, and Value: Introductory Philosophical Dialogues* (Westview Press, 1989).

ABOUT ASEP

ASEP's mission is to provide safe, meaningful, and enjoyable sport experiences for athletes by educating coaches in the areas of coaching philosophy, sport science, sports medicine, and sport techniques and tactics. Sport administrators and parents also play vital roles in shaping sport experiences, and ASEP's curriculum is designed to provide educational resources for all these key players—coaches, parents, sport administrators, and soon, officials—to help them better fulfill their roles.

For up-to-date information on the availability and prices of curricular and other resources, call the ASEP National Center at 800-747-5698, write to us at P.O. Box 5076, Champaign, IL 61825-5076, or e-mail us at asep@hkusa.com. You may also visit ASEP on the World Wide Web at http://www.asep.com/.

ASEP/NFICEP CITIZENSHIP THROUGH SPORTS COURSE

If you've already read *Coaching for Character,* you know you have a valuable tool for developing positive character in your athletes. But reading this book is only the beginning. The real impact will occur when you apply this information to your coaching.

To help you take the next step, the American Sport Education Program (ASEP) and the National Federation of State High School Associations (NFSHSA) have teamed up in their most collaborative project ever to deliver Citizenship Through Sports, an exciting course in the National Federation of Interscholastic Coaches Education Program (NFICEP) that builds upon this book and the NFSHSA's Citizenship Through Sports and Fine Arts curriculum.

Combining active learning exercises, interaction with other coaches, and video support that you can use with your athletes, the Citizenship Through Sports Course helps you teach the fundamentals of good sporting behavior, providing tools and guidance to help you develop citizenship in your athletes by focusing on respect, positive values, proper perspective, sportsmanship, teamwork, healthy lifestyles, community service, and self-evaluation. You'll share ideas with fellow coaches and find enough ideas for developing citizenship to last season after season.

For more information about the Citizenship Through Sports Course, or to find out about clinics near you, call ASEP at 1-800-747-5698, or e-mail asep@hkusa.com. You can also find a schedule of clinics on the Internet at http://www.asep.com/.